O'REILLY®
Strata
Making Data Work

Learn how to turn data into decisions.

From startups to the Fortune 500, smart companies are betting on data-driven insight, seizing the opportunities that are emerging from the convergence of four powerful trends:

- New methods of collecting, managing, and analyzing data

- Cloud computing that offers inexpensive storage and flexible, on-demand computing power for massive data sets

- Visualization techniques that turn complex data into images that tell a compelling story

- Tools that make the power of data available to anyone

Get control over big data and turn it into insight with O'Reilly's Strata offerings. Find the inspiration and information to create new products or revive existing ones, understand customer behavior, and get the data edge.

O'REILLY®

Visit oreilly.com/data to learn more.

Getting Started with Fluidinfo

Nicholas J. Radcliffe and Nicholas H. Tollervey

O'REILLY®

Beijing · Cambridge · Farnham · Köln · Sebastopol · Tokyo

Getting Started with Fluidinfo

by Nicholas J. Radcliffe and Nicholas H. Tollervey

Published by O'Reilly Media, Inc., 1005 Gravenstein Highway North, Sebastopol, CA 95472.

O'Reilly books may be purchased for educational, business, or sales promotional use. Online editions are also available for most titles (*http://my.safaribooksonline.com*). For more information, contact our corporate/institutional sales department: (800) 998-9938 or *corporate@oreilly.com*.

Editors: Andy Oram and Mike Hendrickson	**Cover Designer:** Karen Montgomery
Production Editor: Teresa Elsey	**Interior Designer:** David Futato
	Illustrator: Robert Romano

Revision History for the First Edition:

    2012-02-21   First release

See *http://oreilly.com/catalog/errata.csp?isbn=9781449307097* for release details.

ISBN: 978-1-449-30709-7

[LSI]

1329840422

Table of Contents

Preface vii

1. What Is Fluidinfo? 1
    The Openly Writable World   1
    Key Concepts   2
        Objects   2
        Tags   3
        Users   4
        Permissions   4
        Queries   5
    Organizational Metaphor   6
        Like Wikipedia for Structured Data   6
        Like Delicious for Bookmarking Anything   7
        The About Tag   8
    Signing Up for a Fluidinfo Account   8

2. Fluidinfo from the Command Line 11
    Getting Started with the Tags, Show, and Get Commands   11
    Tagging and Untagging   13
    Specifying Objects   14
    Managing Tags and Namespaces   16
        Listing Files and Namespaces: The ls Command   17
        Removing Tags and Namespaces: The rm Command   18
        Creating Tags and Namespaces: The mkns and touch Commands   20
    The Fluidinfo Permissions System   20
        Listing Permissions on Tags and Namespaces with ls -L   21
        Setting Permissions: Simple Use of the perms Command   22
        Shortcuts for Common Permissions Cases   22
        Setting Group Permissions   23
    Extended Example: Working with Books in Fluidinfo   24

3. **Social Data** **27**
   Twitter and Social Data   27
      Walled Gardens of Data   27
      Tickery: Twitter Data Only   28
      We Met At: Emerging Conventions in Twitter Data   32
      Tunkrank: Adding Value to Twitter Data   33
      A Query Like No Other   33
   O'Reilly Metadata   34
      Instant API   34
      Using the API   35
      Skillshelves: Repurposing and Augmenting O'Reilly Data   37
      A Query Like No Other   38
   Blog Mining and Emerging Conventions   38
      Boing Boing   39
      ReadWriteWeb   40
      Union Square Ventures   41
      A Query Like No Other   41
   Social Data   42

4. **Programming with Fluidinfo** **43**
   Client Libraries   43
      Introducing fluidinfo.py   44
   Fluidinfo.py Fundamentals   45
   Common Tasks Using fluidinfo.py   47
      Create a New Object   47
      Tag an Object with a Value   48
      Get a Specific Value from an Object   49
      Delete a Specific Value from an Object   49
      Query for Specified Values on Matching Objects   50

5. **Programming with FOM** **53**
   FOM Fundamentals   53
      Namespaces and Tags   54
      Working with Objects   56
      Searching Objects   58
      Working with Permissions   59
   Putting It All Together   61

6. **Programming Fluidinfo with JavaScript** **67**
   API Functions   68
      DELETE   69
      GET   70
      HEAD   70

	POST	70
	PUT	71
	Utility Functions	71
	createObject	71
	del	72
	getObject	72
	query	73
	tag	74
	update	74
	An Example Application: The Social Bookreader	75
	Modeling Data: What Is a Book?	75
	Viewing Data: The User Interface	79
	Application Logic: Putting It Together	80
	Next Steps	84

7. Fluidinfo's RESTful API **85**
	Making HTTP Requests to Fluidinfo	85
	User Validation	85
	Request Headers	86
	Response Headers	86
	Encoding	87
	API Endpoints	87
	/about	88
	/namespaces	88
	/objects	89
	/permissions	89
	/tags	90
	/users	90
	/values	91

8. Advanced Use of the Fluidinfo Shell **93**
	Permissions in Depth	93
	Setting Individual Low-Level Permissions with perms -X	96
	Generating Unix-style Long Listings with ls -l and ls -g	97

9. Conventions for the About Tag **99**
	A Book Example	99
	The Perfect About Tag	101
	Normalization and Standardization	102
	Specificity, Ambiguity, and Language	103
	Languages	103
	Tags for Indicating Related Objects (Linking)	104
	Constructing About Tags for Common Objects	107

The Abouttag Command   107
Finding Fluidinfo Objects from Amazon Product Pages   111
Generic Normalization   111
Command Substitution   112

Appendix: Fluidinfo Query Language Reference **113**

Preface

Both the authors became hooked on Fluidinfo through reading obscure material on the Web by its visionary creator, Terry Jones (@terrycojones (*http://twitter.com/terryco jones*)).

Nick Radcliffe (@njr (*http://twitter.com/njr*)) had known Terry from conferences in the late 1980s and early 1990s, when they both did PhDs focusing on representation issues in genetic algorithms. They lost contact for over a decade, but then Radcliffe stumbled upon Terry's personal website, which included a set of papers "rejected by numerous journals and conferences." These discussed information storage and espoused the view that operating systems and the Internet focus on the wrong organizational structure. The papers mapped out a vision in which, rather than being placed in particular locations, data was simply dropped into a storage system and annotated with metadata in the form of attributes that could be used to search, query, relate, and locate different items. From today's perspective, Terry was describing, before they had really been invented, not just tagging in the sense we are familiar with from Delicious, Flickr, and Gmail, but a more sophisticated version where tags could have values and be queried. He coupled this metadata-driven approach with a focus on search that seems unremarkable today, but which was far from mainstream then. Radcliffe got in touch and has been involved in Fluidinfo and its antecedents since then. After two previous abandoned implementations, Terry sold his flat to fund the creation of what has become Fluidinfo, Inc., that company that builds the Fluidinfo software and runs the Fluidinfo service.

Nicholas Tollervey (@ntoll (*http://twitter.com/ntoll*)) first learned of Fluidinfo when Tim O'Reilly (@timoreilly (*http://twitter.com/timoreilly*)) addressed the following tweet to Robert Scoble (@scobleizer (*http://twitter.com/scobleizer*)):

> @Scobleizer Have you connected with @terrycojones? I believe he's in Barcelona, doing really interesting work that ought to be on your radar.[1]

Nicholas watched and rewatched Scoble's four-part video interview (*http://scobleizer .com/2008/12/05/the-unfundable-world-changing-startup/*) with Terry and came to the

---

1. https://twitter.com/timoreilly/statuses/1032592518   (*https://twitter.com/timoreilly/statuses/1032592518*)

conclusion that Terry was either mad or *on to something*. He tracked Terry down and sent him a long email asking for clarification on many aspects of Fluidinfo. He was somewhat surprised, some months later, to receive a detailed and enthusiastic reply from Terry, which also invited him to read the new, very dry Fluidinfo API Reference (*http://api.fluidinfo.com/html/api.html*). Unlikely as it sounds, this confirmed Nicholas's hunch that Terry was on to something and he embarked on a series of "hacks" to explore the capabilities and potential of Fluidinfo. When Fluidinfo gained funding he joined the company as "Guy #3" (*http://sethgodin.typepad.com/seths_blog/2009/06/guy-3.html*).

Organization of this Book

Chapter 1, *What Is Fluidinfo?*, introduces Fluidinfo and covers key concepts at a high level.

Chapter 2, *Fluidinfo from the Command Line*, introduces the Fluidinfo Shell, Fish, a powerful tool for issuing commands directly to Fluidinfo using a simple command language.

Chapter 3, *Social Data*, shows how you can use a variety of web-based applications to read and write Fluidinfo data. It also shows how some of the applications reuse and build upon each other's data.

Chapter 4, *Programming with Fluidinfo*, explores Fluidinfo from the perspective of the software developer. Basic use of the RESTful interface is shown, using the *fluidinfo.py* Python library.

Chapter 5, *Programming with FOM*, introduces developers to a higher-level view of Fluidinfo. The Fluid Object Mapper (FOM) library is introduced to build a simple Python utility.

Chapter 6, *Programming Fluidinfo with JavaScript*, shows an asynchronous programmatic approach using the JavaScript library *fluidinfo.js* to build AJAX web applications.

Chapter 7, *Fluidinfo's RESTful API*, explores Fluidinfo's low-level HTTP API.

Chapter 8, *Advanced Use of the Fluidinfo Shell*, explores advanced uses of Fish and some of the more arcane details of the Fluidinfo permissions system.

Chapter 9, *Conventions for the About Tag*, discusses conventions for the primary identifier used in Fluidinfo, the *about* tag, as well as some more philosophical issues about the design of information architectures.

Finally, Appendix, *Fluidinfo Query Language Reference*, contains a reference guide to the Fluidinfo query language.

Versions

This version of this book documents the version of Fluidinfo with release date 2012-01-10T00:34:00Z, API version 1.14. The release date and API version for the live version of Fluidinfo may be found at *http://fluiddb.fluidinfo.com/about/fluidinfo/fluiddb/release-date* and *http://fluiddb.fluidinfo.com/about/fluidinfo/fluiddb/api-version* respectively. The change log is at *http://doc.fluidinfo.com/fluidDB/api/changelog.html*. The version of Fish documented is version 4.00. The current documentation for Fish is available at *http://fluiddb.fluidinfo.com/about/fish/fish/index.html*.

Conventions Used in This Book

The following typographical conventions are used in this book:

Italic
> Indicates new terms, URLs, email addresses, filenames, and file extensions.

`Constant width`
> Used for program listings, as well as within paragraphs to refer to program elements such as variable or function names, databases, data types, and keywords.

`Constant width bold`
> Shows commands or other text that should be typed literally by the user.

`Constant width italic`
> Shows text that should be replaced with user-supplied values or by values determined by context.

> This icon signifies a tip, suggestion, or general note.

> This icon indicates a warning or caution.

Using Code Examples

This book is here to help you get your job done. In general, you may use the code in this book in your programs and documentation. You do not need to contact us for permission unless you're reproducing a significant portion of the code. For example, writing a program that uses several chunks of code from this book does not require permission. Selling or distributing a CD-ROM of examples from O'Reilly books does require permission. Answering a question by citing this book and quoting example code does not require permission. Incorporating a significant amount of example code from this book into your product's documentation does require permission.

We appreciate, but do not require, attribution. An attribution usually includes the title, author, publisher, and ISBN. For example: "*Getting Started with Fluidinfo* by Nicholas J. Radcliffe and Nicholas H. Tollervey (O'Reilly). Copyright 2012 Nicholas Tollervey, Nicholas Radcliffe, 978-1-449-30709-7."

If you feel your use of code examples falls outside fair use or the permission given above, feel free to contact us at *permissions@oreilly.com*.

Safari® Books Online

Safari Safari Books Online is an on-demand digital library that lets you easily search over 7,500 technology and creative reference books and videos to find the answers you need quickly.

With a subscription, you can read any page and watch any video from our library online. Read books on your cell phone and mobile devices. Access new titles before they are available for print, and get exclusive access to manuscripts in development and post feedback for the authors. Copy and paste code samples, organize your favorites, download chapters, bookmark key sections, create notes, print out pages, and benefit from tons of other time-saving features.

O'Reilly Media has uploaded this book to the Safari Books Online service. To have full digital access to this book and others on similar topics from O'Reilly and other publishers, sign up for free at *http://my.safaribooksonline.com*.

How to Contact Us

Please address comments and questions concerning this book to the publisher:

O'Reilly Media, Inc.
1005 Gravenstein Highway North
Sebastopol, CA 95472
800-998-9938 (in the United States or Canada)
707-829-0515 (international or local)
707-829-0104 (fax)

We have a web page for this book, where we list errata, examples, and any additional information. You can access this page at:

http://shop.oreilly.com/product/0636920020738.do

To comment or ask technical questions about this book, send email to:

bookquestions@oreilly.com

For more information about our books, courses, conferences, and news, see our website at *http://www.oreilly.com*.

Find us on Facebook: *http://facebook.com/oreilly*

Follow us on Twitter: *http://twitter.com/oreillymedia*

Watch us on YouTube: *http://www.youtube.com/oreillymedia*

Acknowledgments

The authors would like to thank the entire Fluidinfo team, not only for creating the system that is this book's focus, but also for responding positively to various requests to change features in time for the book's release. All the members of the team have supported the creation of the book in multiple ways, and we are duly grateful. Terry Jones, in particular, has read multiple drafts of most, if not all chapters, and has our special thanks. We are grateful also to Davison Avery (@otoburb) for giving us detailed feedback on a draft of the book.

We'd also like to thank Andy Oram (@praxagora), our O'Reilly editor, for helping us through and being patient when deadlines, to borrow from Douglas Adams's comment, made that whooshing noise as they went past, and Teresa Elsey (@teresaelsey), for some very sharp copy editing, which tightened up the text considerably.

The book would not have been possible, in its current form, without the work of various people writing libraries and services around Fluidinfo, importing data into it, and generally kicking its tires. If we attempt to mention them all, we will inevitably miss some, but we have to call out specially Ali Afshar (@aliafshar), who wrote the initial implementation of FOM, Sanghyeon Seo (@sanxiyn), who wrote the initial implementation of *Fluidinfo.py*, and Eric Seidel (@gridaphobe), who undertook the gargantuan task of importing a dump of the entire MusicBrainz (public) database to Fluidinfo.

We would also like to thank Becky Hogge (@barefoot_techie). Becky provided an early version of her work Barefoot into Cyberspace (*http://barefootintocyberspace.com/book/*) at a Book Hack Day event in London, the result of which is the web application described in Chapter 6.

Additionally, Nicholas Radcliffe would like to thank both his parents, each of whom read and gave feedback on early drafts of various chapters. Nicholas Tollervey would like to thank his wife, Mary, and their three children, Penelope, Sam, and William, for their ever-cheerful patience and teasing.

CHAPTER 1

What Is Fluidinfo?

Fluidinfo is an online storage system in which there is a place for information about everything—everything that exists, everything that could exist, and everything that can be imagined. It allows anyone to store any information, about anything, in any digital form. And Fluidinfo makes it easy to find information in the system, and to extract it, using an unusually simple query language.

Fluidinfo is a first-class Internet citizen, exposing all its functionality through HTTP, the core protocol that underpins the World Wide Web. Programmers can take advantage of its RESTful API, which makes it easy to integrate with other applications.

Finally, Fluidinfo is social: users can exercise fine control over who can read their data and can even enable other chosen users and applications to write data on their behalf.

The Openly Writable World

One of the key aspects of Web 2.0 was the increasing writability of the Web. Although its inventor, Tim Berners-Lee, always envisaged the Web as openly writable, in its early years there were many more readers than writers. The advent of blogging tools, social networks, user product reviews, and online data services have all contributed to a significant reduction in the asymmetry between Internet authors and consumers. Yet even today, the extent of the Web's writability remains strictly limited.

The motivating concept behind Fluidinfo is to provide a shared data space where anyone can attach granular data of any kind to anything on the Web or *anything in the world*. Of course, physical objects like the Eiffel Tower don't exist on the Web, or in Fluidinfo, so digital data can't literally be attached to them. But the open structure of Fluidinfo and the emerging conventions for how to refer to anything—digital or physical, real or imaginary—offer a very real sense in which Fluidinfo has a nominated container ready to accept information about anything. Any Fluidinfo user can add data to any such container.

Fluidinfo seeks not only to provide a place for arbitrary data, and mechanisms for reading and writing it, but also to leave the creator of that data firmly in control of it. We are all familiar with web services that encourage us to create data inside them, and to import data to them, but which make it much harder to get that data out, still less to allow other applications and services to access it. Fluidinfo takes a different approach: it not only provides excellent mechanisms for extracting and exporting data, but it includes facilities designed to encourage users and applications to share, remix, and reuse data in ways that will often not have been anticipated when it was created. Fundamentally, Fluidinfo leaves the data creator (or owner) in full control, not only in terms of who can read and write that data, but also which *applications* can use, modify, and extend it.

Fluidinfo's radical reimagining of the way data can be created, shared, and controlled online marks a significant departure, which we believe more fully realizes Tim Berners-Lee's original vision of the Web as a read-write medium. This book is a practical guide to several ways to access and use Fluidinfo; we hope it will help you to embrace the writable Web.

Key Concepts

Some systems gain their power through complexity, others through simplicity. Fluidinfo is among the latter. Five core concepts cover most of it:

- *Objects* represent things (real or imaginary).
- *Tags* attach information to objects.
- *Users* use their own tags to attach data to shared objects.
- The *permissions system* controls who can read and write each tag. (Objects do not have owners, so anyone can tag any object.)
- *Queries* select objects by specifying properties of their tags and values. The selected objects can be read or tagged.

Objects

Fluidinfo is a collection of *objects* that function as shared data containers. Data is stored by attaching it to the relevant object using a tag—a kind of digital Post-it note.

Most objects are used to store data about something specific and the object is said to be *about* that thing. It is possible to tell what an object is about in two ways:

- By checking the value of the special, globally unique *about* tag (`fluiddb/about`) attached to the object.[1]

---

1. The selection and meaning of *about* tags are determined by emerging conventions discussed in Chapter 9.

- From the context given by arbitrary tags attached to the object. The *about* tag is the only tag that the system guarantees to be unique and immutable. If you query for objects on the basis of other tags, you may see the tags, and therefore the objects retrieved, change over time.

In some sense Fluidinfo has an object for *everything*. This is reminiscent of Jorge Luis Borges's 1941 story *The Library of Babel,* in which he describes a library containing all the books that could be written. Unfortunately the set of all books that could be written contains far more books full of lies, nonsense, and errors than it does accurate or useful books. The Library of Babel urgently needed a way to find the valuable material.

Most Fluidinfo users are well intentioned, so the quality of information is generally rather higher than in the Library of Babel. Fluidinfo also provides a mechanism to help judge information's trustworthiness by starting every tag with its owner's name. In this way, the system facilitates the establishment of networks of trust.

Tags

Tags attach information to objects.

Fluidinfo users can add data to any object by tagging it. A tag has a name, and its mere presence on an object can carry meaning: Alice might tag books with an `alice/has-read` tag to indicate that she has read them, while Bert might tag things he wishes to acquire with a `bert/wants` tag. Even the *about* tag is owned by a user—the Fluidinfo superuser, `fluiddb`.[2] This is why the full name for the *about* tag is `fluiddb/about`.

Fluidinfo tags can also store data in the form of a *value*, which can be a piece of text, a number, an image, or any other digital information. For example, if Alice likes the book *Alice in Wonderland*, she might add tags with values such as `alice/rating=10` or `alice/comment="I ♥ Lewis Carroll"`, as well as the valueless `alice/has-read`, to Fluidinfo's *Alice in Wonderland* object (Figure 1-1).

Tags whose name starts with `alice` are owned and controlled by Alice (username `alice`). By default, only she can tag objects using her tags, while anyone can read them, but Alice can choose who can read and write her tags on a tag-by-tag basis. Users can assess the trustworthiness of information by examining its provenance and who controls it, which is visible in every tag's name.

The `alice` at the start of all Alice's tags is an example of a *namespace*, which groups tags together in much the same way that a folder groups files together in a file system. Users can create further sub-namespaces if they wish.

---

2. Fluidinfo was originally called FluidDB, and the name of the superuser has not been changed.

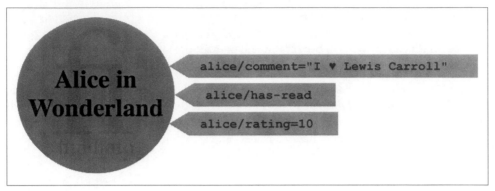

Figure 1-1. The Alice in Wonderland object, with Alice's tags

Users

Anyone can read public data from Fluidinfo without even logging in, but in order to write data you need to authenticate with a valid username and password. Since all Fluidinfo tags are identifiable as being owned by a named user, the system is ideally suited to storing opinions and other personalized data. Because Fluidinfo users can also be applications or organizations (usually using their website's address as a username), the system can also comfortably accommodate application data and institutional data. The permissions system can be used to enable groups of users, or even the entire user base, to have shared write access to tags, allowing data to be formed collaboratively, and in the most extreme cases, in a wiki-like manner.

Permissions

Permissions control who can read and write each tag. They do not apply to objects, leaving Fluidinfo openly writable; in other words, any user can tag any object.

Fluidinfo permissions are expressed in two parts: a policy that is either open or closed and a list of users who are exceptions to the policy.

For example, the *write* permission on the alice/rating tag has a closed policy with one exception—alice herself. As a result, only Alice can tag objects with alice/rating, and only she can remove such tags. In contrast, the *read* permission for the same tag has an open policy with no exceptions, which means that anyone can read Alice's ratings.

Tag permissions can be set programmatically, or using tools such as Fish (Chapter 2) or libraries (see Chapters 4, 5, and 6).

Queries

Fluidinfo has a simple *query language* that makes it easy to find and retrieve information. Many queries look very similar to their description in "natural" English.

Here are some examples of some of the more common types of queries used within Fluidinfo.

Tag presence
> We can select all the objects that have a particular tag with a query like this:
>
> ```
> has alice/rating
> ```
>
> meaning
>> *all the objects that have an* alice/rating *tag attached to them.*

Comparisons
> We can specify numeric values with ordinary equality and inequality tests:
>
> ```
> alice/rating >= 7
> ```
>
> meaning
>> *all the objects that have an* alice/rating *of seven or more.*

Text search
> We can specify words that tag values should contain using the matches operator:
>
> ```
> alice/comment matches "fantastic"
> ```
>
> meaning
>> *all the objects that have an* alice/comment *containing the word "fantastic."*

Multiple conditions
> We can combine any of the previous queries using and, or, and except, adding parentheses as necessary:
>
> ```
> (alice/rating >=7 or alice/comment matches "fantastic") except has alice/owns
> ```
>
> meaning
>> *all the objects that have an* alice/rating *of seven or more or an* alice/comment *that contains "fantastic," other than those with an* alice/owns *tag.*

Users can use any tags they can read in their queries.

A single Fluidinfo query can refer to tags from multiple users. For example, the following query matches all the objects for books that Alice rates highly (6 or more) but that Bert hasn't read:

```
(has alice/books/title and alice/rating >=6) except has bert/has-read
```

(The first clause, has alice/books/title is used here to narrow the set of objects to books Alice knows about, as opposed to all the other things she might rate.)

Organizational Metaphor

As ever more of the world is digitized, the task of managing our data becomes increasingly complex. The overlapping challenges we face include:

- Finding a particular piece of information within our own data
- Keeping data in sync across multiple devices and the Web
- Extracting or integrating data we have stored using different applications and services that may offer little or no support for such export
- Organizing and preserving our data
- Annotating both our own data and information we may not own but can access
- Giving other people and applications appropriate access to our data without losing control of that data

There are many partial solutions to these problems, most of which reduce complexity for the user in exchange for migrating all data to a single place, sometimes with some support for satellite copies. This usually comes at the price of reduced control and flexibility. There are lots of online services that will manage many classes of data for you, and offer good import mechanisms, but once you have exported your digital life to one of these, and perhaps used the tools to annotate and organize the data better, you may find it difficult to reclaim your data.

Fluidinfo grew out of a different vision of how data should be stored and managed. It is not a panacea—the issues involved are probably too complex for any complete technical "solution"—but it does represent a coherent reimagining of the information landscape that speaks to each of these issues with a distinctive voice.

Like Wikipedia for Structured Data

An obvious reference point for Fluidinfo is Wikipedia. In a sense, both Wikipedia and Fluidinfo have a (potential) place for information on any topic. In Wikipedia's case, the repository for a topic is a Wikipedia article, identified by a URL fragment; in the case of Fluidinfo, the repository is an object, and the *about* tag, `fluiddb/about`, acts as the identifier.

The two most fundamental divergences between Wikipedia and Fluidinfo concern *structure* and *point of view*.

Structure
    A Wikipedia page is largely *unstructured* in the technical sense that the information it contains is mostly free-form text, often augmented with images, tables, and other elements designed to be read by a human being. In contrast, the Fluidinfo object is *structured*, typically consisting of a large number of named pieces of information, each having a type. Fluidinfo's query language and API are also relevant differences, but are natural given the more structured nature of Fluidinfo data.

Point of view

An explicitly articulated goal of Wikipedia is to achieve a "neutral point of view (*http://en.wikipedia.org/wiki/Wikipedia:Neutral_point_of_view*)," which is developed through processes of cooperation, collaboration, negotiation, mediation, and (in some cases) edit wars, moderation, and locking. Although a history of changes is maintained, the live Wikipedia page on a topic presents a single version of the truth.

In contrast, all data in Fluidinfo is clearly associated with an owner and different users can all attach their own data to the same shared item. Fluidinfo is very suitable for opinions and other personal data, in a way that Wikipedia is certainly not. Fluidinfo's permissions system provides extra flexibility around data ownership and control.

Because of this key difference, *there are no edit wars in Fluidinfo*.

Like Delicious for Bookmarking Anything

Another reference point for Fluidinfo comes from social bookmarking sites such as Delicious (*http://delicious.com*) and Pinboard (*http://pinboard.in*). These sites provide online storage for bookmarks to web pages, and allow users to organize their bookmarks by attaching any number of simple tags to them. In this context, a tag is just a word, and users normally attach a number of tags to each URL bookmarked to make finding pages on particular subjects easy.

The sense in which these sites are *social* is that, by default, a user's bookmarks are publicly visible. An interesting consequence of this is that searching for pages that many users have tagged with particular terms tends to produce highly relevant results for that term; the degree of coherence of the emergent taxonomic structure (sometimes known as a *tagsonomy*) is remarkable.

Fluidinfo can be viewed as a social bookmarking site in which the bookmarks need not point to web pages but can represent anything (for example, books, songs, films, locations, stocks, Twitter users, people, cars, buildings, taxis, words, concepts, equations, truths, falsehoods, colors, or similes). Fluidinfo further differentiates itself by allowing its tags to have typed values,[3] by providing a query mechanism, by allowing more sophisticated and finer-grained permissions, and by providing a correspondingly more powerful API.

---

3. The note that can be attached to a bookmark in Delicious and Pinboard can be seen as a single example of a special tag with a value in these systems.

The About Tag

As we have seen, where Wikipedia is a collection of collaboratively produced encyclopedia articles, and Delicious is a collection of tagged and annotated URLs, Fluidinfo is a collection of shared objects, each of which represents something.

When an object is created in Fluidinfo, the creator can specify any text as the value of the special tag `fluiddb/about`, which is normally referred to simply as the *about* tag. If an object already exists with the nominated *about* tag, rather than creating a new one, the system reuses the existing object; if the *about* tag doesn't exist, a new object is created. Once created, objects are never destroyed and *about* tags are never changed. As a result, *about* tags act as permanent, unique identifiers for objects, and they are the primary way of specifying objects directly.

Fluidinfo itself attaches no significance to the value of the *about* tag, so the choice of which object to use to store data is left to users and is a matter of convention. In simple cases, such as URLs, the choice is simple and natural—people invariably use the full URL directly as the *about* tag (for example, `fluiddb/about="http://fluidinfo.com"`), though there is slight ambiguity around whether to include a trailing slash (most people do not). In more complex cases, it is important to adopt sensible conventions if you want your data to end up on the same objects as other people's. Such conventions, and tools for helping to construct the conventional *about* tags, are discussed in more detail in Chapter 9.

Signing Up for a Fluidinfo Account

If you want to be able to write data in Fluidinfo, you will need to sign up for an account by visiting Fluidinfo's sign-up page (*https://fluidinfo.com/accounts/new/*). There are two ways to do this. If you have a Twitter account and would like to use the same username in Fluidinfo, just click the "Sign in with Twitter" button and authorize Fluidinfo on Twitter's site; a new Fluidinfo account will be created for you with your Twitter username (if available). If you don't have a Twitter account, or would prefer not to link your accounts, simply supply your name, a unique username (which will identify all of your tags), and a working email address.[4]

Once you've agreed to the terms of use (*http://fluidinfo.com/terms/*) and proved yourself to be human by answering the CAPTCHA[5] Fluidinfo will email you a verification link.

After you have clicked the verification link, your account will be activated.

The next few chapters introduce three different ways of interacting with Fluidinfo. In Chapter 2, we introduce the Fluidinfo Shell, Fish, which provides a mechanism for sending commands directly to Fluidinfo. Then, in Chapter 3, we survey various web

---

4. You can have more than one account associated with a single email address.

5. A type of challenge/response test used to ensure that a response is generated by a person.

applications that use Fluidinfo to store their data. Finally, we show how Fluidinfo can be used programmatically, first from Python (Chapters 4 and 5), then with JavaScript (Chapter 6), and finally directly using the HTTP API (Chapter 7).

 As this book goes to press, Fluidinfo (the company) is just releasing an experimental new interface to Fluidinfo (the storage system) at *http://fluidinfo.com*. This experimental interface is not described in this book at present, because it is in a constant state of flux, often receiving more than one update in a day. We plan to add a chapter describing it when the interface stabilizes.

CHAPTER 2

Fluidinfo from the Command Line

In this chapter we will use a command-line tool, Fish (the Fluidinfo Shell), to interact with Fluidinfo. Fish provides a convenient way to interact with Fluidinfo even if your primary access is programmatic or through a graphical tool such as the Fluidinfo website.

There are two versions of Fish: a convenient web-based application and a more powerful command-line version.

The online version, Shell-Fish (*http://shell-fish.appspot.com*), requires you to log in with a Google account. Once authenticated, go to your settings (*http://shell-fish.appspot .com/settings*) and enter your Fluidinfo username and password. If you haven't done so yet, you can get these by signing up at *http://fluidinfo.com/accounts/new/*, as described in "Signing Up for a Fluidinfo Account" on page 8.

To gain the full power of Fish, you should install it on your system by going to Github (*http://github.com/njr0/fish*), downloading the Python source, and following the instructions in the README file.

Getting Started with the Tags, Show, and Get Commands

Many people store bookmarks to web pages in Fluidinfo, normally using the URL as the *about* tag. For example, Figure 2-1 shows a graphic view of the object with the *about* tag *http://www.chromasia.com/iblog*.

We can use Fish to view all the tags on this object by saying:

```
$ fish tags -a 'http://www.chromasia.com/iblog'
```

 If you are using the online version, the `fish` at the start of each command is unnecessary and can be omitted.

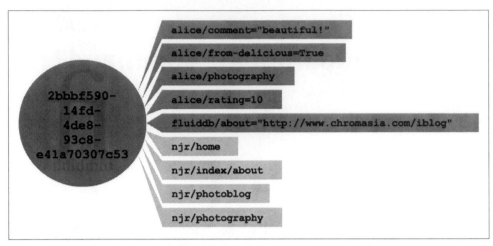

Figure 2-1. The Fluidinfo object for the URL http://www.chromasia.com/iblog

In this line, `tags` is the Fish command to list the tags on an object. The `-a` is called an *option*, and it indicates that we're going to specify the object by using its *about* tag. The argument `http://www.chromasia.org/iblog` indicates the actual *about* tag on the object we want. In this case, it is not strictly necessary to put the *about* tag in quotes, but in general it is a good idea, and it is necessary when the *about* tag contains spaces or certain special characters. The output the command produces should be similar to this:

```
Object with about="http://www.chromasia.com/iblog":
  /alice/comment = "beautiful!"
  /alice/from-delicious = True
  /alice/photography
  /alice/rating = 10
  /njr/home
  /njr/index/about
  /njr/photoblog
  /njr/photography
```

This is fairly self-explanatory, with the first line showing the *about* tag of the object. All the other lines are tags on the object.

The values returned by Fluidinfo have *types*, so that `alice/rating` is a number, `alice/comment` is a textual value (a string), `alice/from-delicious` is a Boolean value (true/false), and all the other tags as are simple tags having no values.[1]

Now that we know the tags on the object, if we just wanted to show a subset of the tags, we could use Fish's `show` command. For example:

```
$ fish show -a 'http://www.chromasia.com/iblog' /alice/rating /alice/comment /about
Object with about="http://www.chromasia.com/iblog":
  /alice/rating = 10
```

---

1. A tag with no value may also be regarded as having a null value: the statements "the tag has no value" and "the tag's value is null" are equivalent in Fluidinfo.

```
/alice/comment = "beautiful!"
/fluiddb/about = "http://www.chromasia.com/iblog"
```

 Note that in general, in Fish, when you specify tag names belonging to users other than yourself, they must be preceded with a leading slash (/). This is to allow you to omit your name from your own tags. So Alice can refer to her rating tag as `rating`, but if she wants to refer to Bert's `rating` tag, she specifies it as `/bert/rating`. Fish removes the leading slashes before sending tags to Fluidinfo and adds the user's namespace where necessary. The only exception to these rules is when specifying queries, with the `-q` option, as will be explained later.

There are also two special abbreviations. The *about* tag (`fluiddb/about`) may be referenced as `/about`, and the object's ID (`fluiddb/id`) as `/id`.[2]

Fish's `get` command is the same as `show`, except that it doesn't include the tag's name in the output, which is sometimes more convenient when scripting:

```
$ fish get -a 'http://www.chromasia.com/iblog' /alice/rating
10
```

Tagging and Untagging

The fundamental operations in Fluidinfo are *tagging* (adding tags, often with values, to one or more objects), *untagging* (removing tags from objects), and *retrieving* tags and their values from objects. Fish uses commands called `tag` and `untag` for the first two of these, and has four commands for retrieving tags: in addition to `show`, `get`, and `tags`, which we have seen, there is the `count` command, which simply counts the number of objects that satisfy some criteria.

The command Alice used to write a tag to *http://www.chromasia.com/iblog* with her rating of 10 was

```
$ fish tag -a 'http://www.chromasia.com/iblog' rating=10
```

The command produces no output when it is successful. Multiple tags can be specified at the same time. For example,

```
$ fish tag -a 'http://www.chromasia.com/iblog' rating=10 comment='Beautiful!'
from-delicious=true photography
```

In this example, the first three tags (`rating`, `comment`, and `from-delicious`) all have values of various types, and the last tag, `photography`, is a plain tag with no value.

---

2. Actually, `fluiddb/id` is a *pseudo*-tag. Although all Fluidinfo objects have a `fluiddb/id` tag, and can be accessed through the API via their ID, `fluiddb/id` can only be queried in a restricted way, as we will see.

If values are being specified, they should follow an equals sign with no surrounding spaces. In general, Fish interprets values that look like numbers as numeric values (even if they are quoted), interprets `True` and `False` as Boolean values (regardless of capitalization), and interprets anything else as a string. If the text contains spaces or nonalphanumeric characters, it should usually be quoted.

Tags are removed with the `untag` command. For example, Alice could remove her `rating` and her `comment` from *http://www.chromasia.com/iblog* by entering

```
$ fish untag -a 'http://www.chromasia.com/iblog' rating comment
```

If you haven't already done so, try tagging and untagging some URLs with your own `rating` or `comment` tags, or whatever else you like, remembering that for valueless tags you can just use words without any `=value` part, as with the `photography` tag in the `tag` command above. Most URLs in Fluidinfo are specified in the form browsers show them, which means that they include the `http://` at the start, and that top-level domains usually include a trailing slash. You will be more likely to use the same object as others if you follow that convention, and since the paradigm for information sharing in Fluidinfo is to attach different tags to the same object, this is desirable.

Specifying Objects

The reason we need to use the `-a` option to tell Fish that we want to specify objects by giving their `about` tags is that there are two other options. Objects can be specified by ID (`-i`), or by matching with a Fluidinfo query (`-q`).

We saw from in Figure 2-1 that the ID for the object corresponding to the web page `http://www.chromasia.com/iblog` is `2bbbf590-14fd-4de8-93c8-e41a70307c53`. This being the case, any of the commands issued so far could be modified to replace the `-a 'http://www.chromasia.com/iblog'` option with `-i 2bbbf590-14fd-4de8-93c8-e41a70307c53`. For example, the `untag` command shown previously could be reformulated as

```
$ fish untag -i 2bbbf590-14fd-4de8-93c8-e41a70307c53 rating comment
```

You can use any of the commands we have seen so far to operate on *all* the objects that match a given query by using the `-q` option followed by the Fluidinfo query specification. Fish does not process the query itself, but passes it directly to Fluidinfo. For this reason, within queries, all tags must be referenced in the normal full-path fashion (for example, `alice/rating`), even the user's own tags, and no leading slashes are used.

A full specification of the Fluidinfo Query Language is given in the Appendix. Here are a few examples. As mentioned earlier, the `count` command returns the number of objects that match a given query:

```
$ fish count -q 'has alice/rating'
11 objects matched
Total: 11 objects
```

Here the query is `has alice/rating`, which matches all objects that have an `alice/rating` tag attached to them, regardless of its value. We use the Fish `count` command to find the number of objects that match the query.

 The Fluidinfo API does not provide functionality for counting the number of objects that match a given query, so Fish retrieves the IDs of all the matching objects that match and counts them before discarding them. If the number of matching objects is very large, the count operation may be slow. If you are using the online Shell-Fish version, very large counts may cause the application to time out (if it takes more than 10 seconds to get the IDs from Fluidinfo).

Another common use of queries is to find objects matching a condition:

```
$ fish show -q 'has alice/rating' /about /alice/rating
11 objects matched
Object 1529c459-f3f2-45e1-90f4-3ff3040ad6df:
  /fluiddb/about = "book:animal farm (george orwell)"
  /alice/rating = 2
Object d135729f-5005-4c7b-833c-360480e73e05:
  /fluiddb/about = "alice's adventures in wonderland"
  /alice/rating = 11
Object d78d4272-ea31-43ff-bd5e-ee52e9a42a87:
  /fluiddb/about = "album:led zeppelin iv (led zeppelin)"
  /alice/rating = 5
Object f367a03f-4d03-4f05-ac19-2456339d4f82:
  /fluiddb/about = "through the looking-glass"
  /alice/rating = 11
Object adb59d27-6f1b-4c54-a319-7d895cff9036:
  /fluiddb/about = "book:les misérables (victor hugo)"
  /alice/rating = 2
Object 03c8ce35-aa5e-4b58-b3ab-ddda55642b15:
  /fluiddb/about = "book:alices adventures in wonderland (lewis carroll)"
  /alice/rating = 10
Object 1fb8e9cb-70b9-4bd0-a7e7-880247384abd:
  /fluiddb/about = "DADGAD"
  /alice/rating = 10
Object 5552677a-ea70-4991-adbb-c0973f90f09b:
  /fluiddb/about = "http://durhamtownship.com/"
  /alice/rating = 10
Object 352f7fb0-0237-4372-aab4-33fe2f18297c:
  /fluiddb/about = "book:emma (jane austen)"
  /alice/rating = 8
Object 2bbbf590-14fd-4de8-93c8-e41a70307c53:
  /fluiddb/about = "http://www.chromasia.com/iblog"
  /alice/rating = 10
Object 17ecdfbc-c148-41d3-b898-0b5396ebe6cc:
  /fluiddb/about = "Paris"
  /alice/rating = "smelly"
```

Similarly, we can find things Alice has rated "smelly" with this query:

```
$ fish show -q 'alice/rating="smelly"' /about
1 object matched
Object 17ecdfbc-c148-41d3-b898-0b5396ebe6cc:
  /fluiddb/about = "Paris"
```

 The quoting shown is appropriate for Unix-like systems and for the online version of Fish (Shell-Fish). On Windows, single quotes do not work and double quotes should be used instead.

Since the query language expects text to be quoted using double quotes, and since Windows uses double quotes to quote text, we will need to include double quotes within double quotes. The Windows mechanism for this is *stuttering* (in other words, repeating the quote). Thus on Windows, this command becomes

```
$ fish show -q "alice/rating=""smelly""" /about
```

Finally we will look at a query with multiple conditions. This one picks out items that Alice has tagged with her photography tag and has rated 10:

```
$ fish show -q 'has alice/photography and alice/rating=10' /about
2 objects matched
Object 2bbbf590-14fd-4de8-93c8-e41a70307c53:
  /fluiddb/about = "http://www.chromasia.com/iblog"
Object 5552677a-ea70-4991-adbb-c0973f90f09b:
  /fluiddb/about = "http://durhamtownship.com/"
```

Managing Tags and Namespaces

The structure of a user's tag hierarchy is very similar to the structure of a user's filespace on a computer—a Unix file system in particular. In this analogy, Fluidinfo namespaces map to file-system directories (folders) and Fluidinfo tags map to files. In the context of a particular object, you can even regard the value of a tag as being analogous to the contents of a file.

Fish deliberately exploits this analogy and models most of its commands for managing tags and namespaces on the corresponding Unix commands. Thus, Fish provides an ls command (*list sorted*) to list tags and namespaces, an rm command (*remove*) for deleting them, and some less commonly used commands—mkns for *making namespaces* and touch for creating tags. The mkns and touch commands are rarely needed because tags and namespaces are created automatically when they are first used, but there are sometimes reasons to use them. Fish also allows mkdir to be used as an synonym for mkns, as a concession to Unix users, who are used to typing mkdir.

The main departure from direct analogues to Unix command names is Fish's command for setting permissions, which is perms rather than chmod. Fluidinfo's permissions model, and consequently its rules for setting permissions, is sufficiently different from the ones used by Unix that using the same command name would probably be unhelpful. The `ls` command can, however, list permissions in a way fairly similar to that used on Unix, with the `-l` and `-g` options.

 A small but significant difference between Fluidinfo and Unix lies in their handling of paths. In Unix, full ("absolute") paths begin with a leading slash (for example, */home/alice/mailbox*) and paths without this leading slash are interpreted by Unix shells as being relative to a *current working directory* (`cwd`), which is set to the user's home directory at login and which may then be changed. In Fluidinfo, "full" paths have no leading slash and there is normally no notion of a relative path. *All paths are absolute in Fluidinfo.*

Because it is so common for users to want to access tags in their own namespace, Fish adopts a Unix-like convention by assuming that any tags mentioned are in the user's own top-level namespace unless they are explicitly introduced with a leading slash. So for Alice, `rating` is her rating tag (`alice/rating`), but she must refer to Bert's rating tag as `/bert/rating`.

Note, however, that when queries are used to specify objects (using the `-q` flag), the query text is passed unmodified to Fluidinfo; therefore, full Fluidinfo-style paths, with no leading slash, should be used for all tags in queries. Although this may be confusing at first, it is very easy to get used to as long as you remember that the leading slash and relative paths are provided by Fish just for convenience.

Listing Files and Namespaces: The ls Command

Fish's `ls` command lists tags and namespaces. If no parameters are given, the user's top-level namespace is listed, so that if the user is authenticated as Alice, this might be the result:

```
$ fish ls
comment            has-read            rating
favourite-things   private/            to-read
```

Namespaces are shown with a trailing /, and all names are relative to the namespace being listed.

One or more namespaces or tags may be listed by specifying their paths after the command. For example, to list the contents of her `private` namespace, Alice could use this command:

```
$ fish ls private
fears      has-drunk
```

The `-r` option can be used to get Fish to recurse, showing the contents of all sub-namespaces, sub-sub-namespaces, and so forth:

```
$ fish ls -r
```

```
alice:
comment              has-read         rating
favourite-things     private/         to-read

alice/private:
fears       has-drunk
```

 Recursive descent options: Although Fish generally strives to be as consistent with standard Unix commands as is reasonable, Unix itself is wildly inconsistent about whether the option for specifying recursive descent is -r or -R. In Fish, these can be used interchangeably.

The ls command also supports -l, -L, -g, and -G options, which trigger various forms of longer listings that include information about permissions, as well as -n and -d options, both of which instruct Fish to list information about the namespace itself, rather than its contents. These versions of the command are discussed in "The Fluidinfo Permissions System" on page 20.

 Fish does not support globbing at this time (in other words, wildcards such as * and ? have no effect within Fish). If you regularly need to use wildcard characters in arguments to Fish, consider using an interactive Fish session. You can start such a session by entering fish with no parameters. This has advantages on both Unix and Windows, though the benefits are different. On Unix, because the (Unix) shell does not process the commands in an interactive Fish session, its wildcard expansion is not a factor. On Windows, when running interactively you are able to use single quotes and avoid the need to stutter double quotes. Exit the interactive session with Ctrl-D on Unix, Ctrl-Z on Windows.

 Case sensitivity: Fluidinfo is, in general, sensitive to capitalization, but usernames may be specified in any case. Usernames will always be returned as lowercase by Fluidinfo. This is similar to the way URLs work: the domain name part is case-insensitive, but the rest of the URL is not (though this actually depends on the web server involved).

Removing Tags and Namespaces: The rm Command

Fish's rm command removes tags and namespaces. In its simplest form, provided that the tags are not in use, the tags or namespaces specified are simply annihilated. In this context, a tag is considered to be in use if it is attached to any objects,[3] and a namespace is considered to be in use if it is not empty. For example, Alice could remove her private namespace and her rating tag, if they were not in use, by entering

```
$ fish rm private rating
```

There is no output if the removal is successful.

The requirement for a tag not to be in use for it to be removed without *forcing* is a protection mechanism implemented by Fish. The Fluidinfo API will happily allow you to remove a tag from a million objects with a single HTTP DELETE operation. So it's not so much a case of *caveat emptor* as *caveat actor*.

More commonly, `rm` is used with tags and namespaces that *are* in use. In these cases, extra options must be used to force Fish to perform its more destructive operations. The `-r` option can be used to specify *recursive descent*, which will cause anything in a namespace being removed to be deleted before the namespace is annihilated. Additionally, the `-f` option can be used to *force* tags that are in use to be removed; this naturally results in the removal of the tag from all objects. As in Unix, these options are commonly used in combination, and can be specified together as `-rf`. Thus Alice could remove her `private` namespace, together with the tags it contains and all of the occurrences of those tags on objects by entering the following:

```
$ rm -rf private
```

If Alice omitted the `-r` flag, the deletion would fail because the private directory would not be empty:

```
$ rm private
Fish failure:
   Error Status 412 (PRECONDITION_FAILED (probably not empty)); [/alice/private]
```

(In this case the `-f` is not strictly required, but it does no harm). Similarly, if Alice tried to remove her `rating` tag when it was still attached to one or more objects, she would get an error:

```
$ rm rating
Fish failure:
   Error Status 412 (PRECONDITION_FAILED (probably not empty)); [/alice/rating]
```

As in Unix, a side effect of the `-f` flag is that is suppresses warnings if the items to be removed do not exist. So whereas if Alice tried to remove a nonexistent tag `cheshire` without the flag, she would get a failure message:

```
$ rm cheshire
Fish failure:
   No tag or namespace found for: cheshire
```

if she adds the `-f` flag there will be no complaint:

---

3. In Unix, of course, a file does not have to be empty to be removed using `rm -r`, so it might seem odd to insist that a tag not be in use for simple removal with Fish's `rm` command. The key difference is that in Unix, even though a single file may be large, it is a single item, whereas in Fluidinfo a tag may be attached to a million objects. It therefore seems reasonable to require the user to confirm that the intention really is to remove all instances of the tag when it is in use; as we shall see, this is easily achieved using the `-f` ("force") option.

```
$ rm -f cheshire
$
```

Be aware that there are no *undo* operations in Fish (or Fluidinfo), so it is wise not to get into the habit of using -rf unthinkingly.

 On Unix, the -f option also forces removals to be carried out in cases where they are forbidden by permissions, provided that the user is permitted to alter those permissions. This is not yet the case in Fish, though it is likely that in future the option's power will be increased to provide this functionality.

Creating Tags and Namespaces: The mkns and touch Commands

It is not necessary to create tags or namespaces before using them in Fluidinfo.[4] Nevertheless, a user may wish to create them explicitly either to set their permissions before use or to set their descriptions.

The touch command creates a tag, if it doesn't already exist. For example,

```
$ fish touch -d 'between 0 (worst) and 5 (best)' star-rating
```

will create a tag star-rating and set its description. The command has no effect if the tag already exists (not even changing its description).

Similarly, a namespace can be created with the command

```
$ fish mkns books
```

which again has no effect if the namespace already exists, and which, like touch, accepts a -d option to set a description. The synonym mkdir can be used instead of mkns (because Fish would be lying if it claimed not to understand the user's intention in that case).

The Fluidinfo Permissions System

Fluidinfo has a powerful and flexible permissions system that governs who can read and write each tag and namespace, and also who can set the permissions for tags and namespaces. A permission consists of a *policy*, which can be either open or closed, and an *exception list*, which is a list of Fluidinfo users for whom the policy is reversed. As an example, there is a permission that controls who can tag things with Alice's rating tag. By default, this permission will be set to

```
policy: closed; exceptions=[alice]
```

---

4. Fluidinfo will automatically create a tag the first time it is attached to an object, together with any namespaces in its path. Such automatically created tags and namespaces have no descriptions.

Here, *closed* means that the action (tagging things with `alice/rating`) is not generally available, but because Alice is on the exception list, the policy is reversed for her. So Alice alone is able to tag things with `alice/rating`.

As you might expect, the default setting for all write permissions is `closed` except for the owner[5] of the tag or namespace. The same is true for *control* permissions, which govern who can change the permissions on the tag or namespace in question. Read permissions, on the other hand, are open by default, with an empty exception list. As a result, anyone can read any Fluidinfo data that has not had its access restricted.

Although conceptually simple, permissions can become quite involved, so we will work through various aspects of them in turn. We will begin with a simplified view of permissions that covers the overwhelming majority of real-world use cases, and we will then move on to explore them in glorious detail.

Listing Permissions on Tags and Namespaces with ls -L

Alice can list the permissions on her top-level namespace by entering either `ls -Ld` or `ls -Ld /alice` (recall that the `-d` and `-n` options tell Fish to list the namespace itself, rather than the tags and namespaces within it):

```
$ fish ls -Ld

alice/:
     read: policy: open; exceptions = []
    write: policy: closed; exceptions = [alice]
  control: policy: closed; exceptions = [alice]
```

 In order to view permissions on a tag or namespace, a user must have *control* permission for it. In practice, this normally means that users can view permissions only on their own tags and namespaces. The reader will not be able to look at permissions on Alice's namespace or tags because Alice is far too sensible to grant others control over her things.

Similarly, Alice can list the permissions on her **rating** tag like this:

```
$ fish ls -L rating

alice/rating:
     read: policy: open; exceptions = []
    write: policy: closed; exceptions = [alice]
  control: policy: closed; exceptions = [alice]
```

---

5. In this book, we always use *owner* to mean the user in whose top-level namespace a tag or namespace sits. It is possible, in Fluidinfo, to transfer control of a tag or namespace to one or more Fluidinfo users other than the owner, but we consider that to be a change of *control*, rather than of ownership.

Setting Permissions: Simple Use of the perms Command

Fish provides a `perms` command for setting permissions on tags and namespaces. In terms of the permissions we have seen so far, each individual permission class (read, write, or control) can be set individually, but there are also shortcuts allowing common settings to be achieved with minimum hassle. We illustrate both.

Suppose Alice wants to set her `private/fears` tag so that Bert and her Greek friend Γλαύκων (username **γλαύκων**) can read it and so that Bert can write it. She can achieve this as follows:

```
$ fish perms read closed except alice+bert+γλαύκων private/fears
$ fish perms write closed except alice+bert private/fears
$ ls -L private/fears

alice/private/fears:
      read: policy: open; exceptions = [alice, bert, γλαύκων]
     write: policy: closed; exceptions = [alice, bert]
   control: policy: closed; exceptions = [alice]
```

Whenever a list of users is to be specified in Fish, a plus-separated list is used—for example, **alice+bert**. If the list consists of a single user, the naked username is used (for example, **bert**). There should be no spaces around the + separator.

If there are no exceptions, the `except…` part is simply omitted. So to set her `private/fears` tag back to being world-readable, Alice could enter this:

```
$ fish perms read open private/fears
```

When a new tag or sub-namespace is created, its permissions are set based on the permissions of its parent namespace. In this way, tags and namespaces created within a restricted namespace inherit the relevant restrictions. It is important to understand, however, that the permissions system is not hierarchical: changing a namespace's permissions has no effect on tags and namespaces already in existence under it. Setting the read permissions on Alice's `private` namespace to `closed except [alice]` will not stop people reading existing tags and sub-namespaces within it if they could previously see those: the permissions on each tag will have to be changed as well to achieve this.

All newly created Fluidinfo accounts include a sub-namespace called `private` with its permissions set to allow only the owner to read, write, and control it. The inheritance of permissions when tags and namespaces are created means that, unless permissions are explicitly changed, it is safe to assume that all data under a user's private namespace will be private.

Shortcuts for Common Permissions Cases

The `perms` command provides shortcuts for common permissions settings. These are the simplest four cases:

private
> Sets a tag or namespace so that only its owner can read, write, and control it. In Alice's case, this means setting all permissions to `closed` except `[alice]`.

default
> Sets a tag or namespace so that only its owner can write and control it, but anyone can read it.

lock
> Removes all write permissions from everyone, protecting the tag or namespace (in other words, write permissions become `closed` with an empty exception list). Using `lock` does not alter read or control permissions.

unlock
> Sets the write permissions to be closed with the exception of the owner. Like `lock`, `unlock` does not change control or read permissions.

The form of the command is simple:

```
fish perms spec list-of-tags-and-namespaces
```

where *spec* is `private`, `default`, `lock`, or `unlock`.

For example, Alice might remove all write permissions from her `private` namespace by entering this command:

```
$ fish perms lock private
```

Setting Group Permissions

The next most common case is to allow a group of users (as well as the owner) to read or write a tag or namespace while excluding everyone else. This is achieved using the `group-read`, `group-write`, or `group` shortcuts, together with a plus-separated list of usernames.

In the first case, assume Alice wants to allow Bert and Γλαύκων to read her `private-fears`. She would enter this:

```
$ fish perms group-read bert+γλαύκων private/fears
```

It doesn't matter whether Alice includes herself on the list: the `group` forms of the `perms` command always grant the owner access.

Similarly, if she wanted to allow Bert (but not Γλαύκων) to write this tag, she could use this command:

```
$ fish perms group-write bert private/fears
```

Finally, if she decided she wanted to allow both Bert and Γλαύκων to read and write the tag, she could use this single command:

```
$ fish perms group bert+γλαύκων
  private/fears
```

Extended Example: Working with Books in Fluidinfo

There is more detail on Fish in Chapter 8, but we will finish this chapter by looking at a slightly more complex example of a kind of data often stored in Fluidinfo, namely books.

Books are often stored in Fluidinfo using *about* tags that follow the book-u (*http://blog .abouttag.com/2011/04/pretty-good-uniqueness.html*) convention, in which books are identified by text of this general form:

```
book:title (author)
```

with the title and author mapped to lowercase and standardized by removing most punctuation and regularizing spacing. You can use Fish's about book command to find *about* tags. Any string that has embedded spaces should be enclosed in single or double quotation marks, so Fish knows it is a single argument. For example:

```
$ fish about book 'Animal Farm' 'George Orwell'
book:animal farm (george orwell)
$ fish about book 'La Bête Humaine' 'Émile Zola'
book:la bête humaine (émile zola)
$ fish about book "The Hitchhiker's Guide to the Galaxy" "Douglas Adams"
book:the hitchhikers guide to the galaxy (douglas adams)
```

Without worrying about the full details for now, these are the basic elements of the convention:

- The *about* tag starts with book:.
- This is followed immediately by the title of the book, exactly as it appears on the book, mapped to lowercase, with some punctuation removed but with accents preserved.
- The book title is followed by a single space and then the name of the author, exactly as it appears on the book, in parentheses. The author is normalized in the same way as the title (mapped to lowercase, preserving accents, and stripping most punctuation).

Let's see now what tags there are on *Animal Farm*. To do this, use this command:

```
$ fish tags -a 'book:animal farm (george orwell)'
Object with about="book:animal farm (george orwell)":
  alice/comment="So disappointing."
  alice/has-read
  alice/likes=false
  alice/rating = 2
  bert/comment="What a book: I love it!"
  bert/has-read
  bert/rating = 8
  fluiddb/about = "book:animal farm (george orwell)"
  miro/class = "record"
  miro/books/author = "George Orwell"
  miro/books/surname = "Orwell"
  miro/books/title = "Animal Farm"
```

```
njr/rating = 10
njr/index/about
miro/books/forename = "George"
miro/books/guardian-1000 = True
miro/books/year = 1945
girafind/books/author = ['George Orwell']
girafind/books/language = "["$_english"]"
girafind/books/title = "Animal Farm"
```

This is the command Alice used to write a tag to *Animal Farm* with her rating of 2:

```
$ fish tag -a 'book:animal farm (george orwell)' rating=2
```

We can avoid needing to specify the *about* tag directly by using command substitution, which is discussed in detail in Chapter 8. Essentially this allows us to use the output from one command as part of another. The exact form depends on which platform Fish is being used on, but in the online version (Shell-Fish), the following works:

```
alice> tag -a "`about book 'Animal Farm' 'George Orwell'`" rating=2
```

The command within left quotes (about book 'Animal Farm' 'George Orwell') is executed first, producing the output book:animal farm (george orwell), which is then used as the -a parameter.

Try tagging some books. First generate the appropriate *about* tag using fish about book, then tag it. (The object for the book does not have to exist in advance.) Alternatively, the About Tag (*http://blog.abouttag.com*) blog has a list of *The Guardian*'s "1000 books that everyone should read" (*http://blog.abouttag.com/2010/03/how-to-tag-books -in-fluiddb.html*); you will probably find a fair number of books on this list that you have already read. Fluidinfo's miro user has tagged these with, among other things, author (miro/books/author), title (miro/books/title), and publication year (miro/ books/year). They also all have a miro/books/guardian-1000 tag (with value True), which can be used for matching.

CHAPTER 3

Social Data

What is social data?

From Fluidinfo's perspective, it is data from many easily discernible sources that, by virtue of the *way it is stored*, can be shared, repurposed, enhanced, annotated, augmented, and easily queried in an environment that encourages open participation.

This chapter aims to show the benefits of publishing social data. The following topics will be of particular interest:

- How different sources map their data to Fluidinfo
- Conventions that have emerged for organizing data
- How data is shared, reused, and enhanced between different sources and applications

Three different domains of data will be used to explore these issues: social networking data based on Twitter, O'Reilly's book catalog, and articles from some technology-related blogs.

Twitter and Social Data

Twitter, because of its popularity and influence, boasts one of the most "crunched" datasets on the Internet. Dozens of services, public and for hire, process Twitter data. But metadata about Twitter users and tweets is not widely shared, and in this section we'll show how Fluidinfo can expose interesting facts about Twitter's use.

Walled Gardens of Data

Twitter (*http://twitter.com*)[1] is a social networking site whose users *tweet* messages of no more than 140 characters in length. Users *follow* one another in order to subscribe

---

1. Given the probable readership of this book, explaining Twitter is likely to be redundant. Nevertheless, we've included an explanation for the sake of the author's parents.

to one another's streams of tweets. Millions of users around the world share tweets about every imaginable subject.

Twitter's API allows developers to get at the service's data. For example, it is possible to find out who follows whom; the most recent 2,000 tweets a user has made; and information such as the name, the "avatar" (the image associated with an account), and the description a user has assigned to himself.

Such a profusion of information about users' friendships, opinions, habits, and influence has generated many third-party services. These services attempt to create value by mining the data, analyzing it, and then making the results available to their users. Unfortunately, the status quo is that Twitter and its satellite services exist as walled gardens of data, hidden in different databases behind a profusion of websites and inconsistent APIs.

Ironically, for a social network, Twitter's data is not *social* in the Fluidinfo sense. This problem has been remarked upon at various times during Twitter's short but eventful life. A typical comment is this tweet from 2009 by Internet luminary Nova Spivack:

> Idea: make a page for every tweet's message_id. On it, put metadata about the tweet. Anyone *[sic]* app can add metadata about/for that id. #newnet[2]

His idea for an openly writable place to store and share data already exists in the form of an object in Fluidinfo, whose *about* value is the URL to the specific tweet. Furthermore, since there can be objects for any *thing* in Fluidinfo, there are also objects about Twitter users and hashtags.[3]

Several applications store and use Twitter-derived data in Fluidinfo. By doing so, they have the opportunity to reuse one another's data. The following are some of the more interesting examples.

Tickery: Twitter Data Only

Tickery (*http://tickery.net/*) was created as a demonstration application by Fluidinfo founder Terry Jones. It has two aims:

- To import interesting data about Twitter users into Fluidinfo
- To provide a user interface for exploring who follows whom

Tickery represents each Twitter user with an object whose *about* value is the user's Twitter name (in its @ form; for example, @ntoll).[4]

---

2. https://twitter.com/novaspivack/statuses/4999653280   (*https://twitter.com/novaspivack/statuses/ 4999653280*)

3. Hashtags are an informal *ad hoc* means of self-classifying tweets with single words prepended with the *hash* (#) sign. For example, #newnet in Nova Spivack's tweet.

4. In any problem domain, if it's possible to name things with proper nouns, you probably want to map such things to objects in Fluidinfo.

Since all the data is from Twitter, Tickery uses the tags created by the `twitter.com` user.[5]

Within the `twitter.com` namespace[6] are two further namespaces, `twitter.com/friends` and `twitter.com/users` (see Figure 3-1).

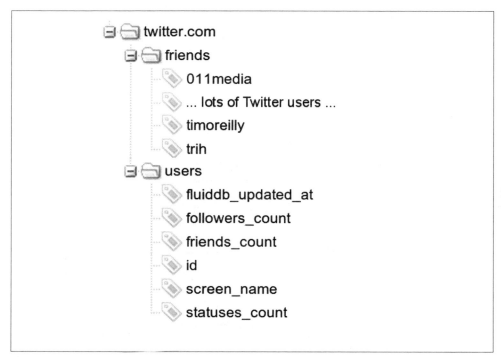

Figure 3-1. The twitter.com namespace/tag schema

The `twitter.com/friends` namespace contains a tag for each user who has imported his or her Twitter data into Fluidinfo. If Terry (@terrycojones on Twitter) is followed by Nicholas (@ntoll on Twitter), a tag called `twitter.com/friends/ntoll` indicating this relationship will be attached to the object representing the Twitter user @terryco jones. Similarly, if Terry also follows Nicholas, a `twitter.com/friends/terrycojones` tag will be attached to the object representing the Twitter user @ntoll.

The `twitter.com/users` namespace contains tags that describe Twitter users:

5. Terry has used his privilege as the creator of Fluidinfo to store tags as the `twitter.com` user. It's important to note that Fluidinfo *normally only allows the owners of a domain to use the domain name as a username* and this use of `twitter.com` is most definitely an exception.

6. Remember, tags are organized in directory-like structures called *namespaces*. Namespaces give tags meaning and context. Namespaces can contain other namespaces or tags and everyone starts with an empty namespace that has the same name as his or her username (which is why all a user's tags start with his or her username: `alice/rating` means the `rating` tag in the `alice` namespace).

`twitter.com/users/fluiddb_updated_at`
> The last time the user's data was updated/imported from Twitter into Fluidinfo

`twitter.com/users/followers_count`
> The number of followers a user has

`twitter.com/users/friends_count`
> The number of friends (people the user is following) a user has

`twitter.com/users/id`
> The unique Twitter ID number for a user

`twitter.com/users/screen_name`
> A user's name on Twitter

`twitter.com/users/statuses_count`
> The number of times the user has tweeted

Tickery uses this very simple schema for representing Twitter users and their followers and leverages Fluidinfo's search capabilities to deliver powerful and unique ways of exploring users' relationships within Twitter (the so-called social graph). Tickery introduces these capabilities with three "modes": *simple*, *intermediate*, and *advanced*.

In the *simple* mode, (Figure 3-2), users just enter two Twitter usernames and click a button. The result is a set of all the Twitter users that the two specified users both follow in common. Hovering over each user in the results allows you to find out more information about him or her.

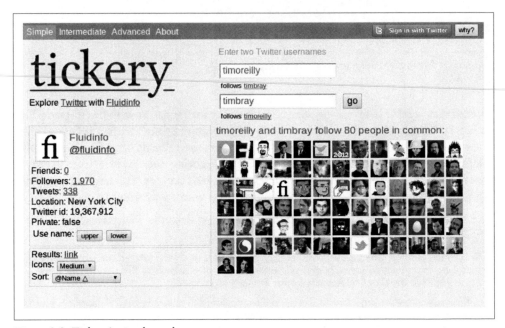

Figure 3-2. Tickery's simple mode

The *intermediate* mode expects you to ask Tickery interesting questions in order to match Twitter followers. This is done with an easy-to-use yet powerful Twitter-specific query language.

Entering a Twitter username will return a list of the people that user follows, so simply entering `ntoll` will list all the people Nicholas follows.

It's also possible to use the logical operators **and**, **or**, and **except** to combine results from more than one user. For example, typing in the query

```
ntoll and terrycojones
```

will return all the people they follow in common. Similarly, using **or** will return users followed by either `ntoll` or `terrycojones` (or both). Using **except** excludes sets of people followed. For example,

```
ntoll except terrycojones
```

returns people Nicholas follows who are not followed by Terry.

Parenthesis are used for grouping, so that the query

```
ntoll except (terrycojones or esteve)
```

will get back all of the people Nicholas is following, except those that either Terry or Esteve follow (Figure 3-3).

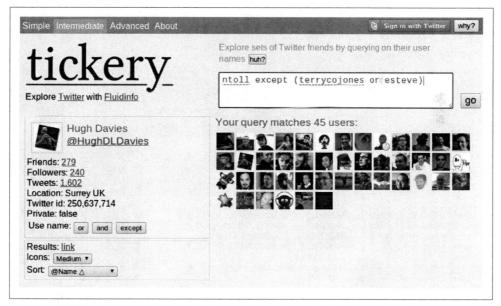

Figure 3-3. Tickery's intermediate mode (note the use of a simple domain-specific language)

Finally, the *advanced* mode lets you submit queries using the raw Fluidinfo query language. Importantly, because this is not Twitter-specific, you can write queries using tags beyond the scope of the `twitter.com` namespace.

How is this useful? Consider that many Fluidinfo users have created a met tag in their top-level namespace. They attach it to objects representing other users whom they've met in real life. As a result, queries such as

```
has terrycojones/met and has
    twitter.com/friends/terrycojones
```

become possible. Twitter data becomes easy to combine with *ad hoc* user-generated data (more on this below).

We Met At: Emerging Conventions in Twitter Data

The We Met At (*http://wemet.at*) web application makes use of the met tagging convention described above. Users sign in to Fluidinfo and then select a Twitter user whose followers are listed. Clicking on a follower displays information about the selected Twitter user and includes a single checkbox to allow the logged-in Fluidinfo user to indicate whether they've met in real life.

That's it.

As Figure 3-4 shows, Nicholas (ntoll on Fluidinfo) has retrieved all the Twitter followers of his @ntoll Twitter account, selected Nick's @njr Twitter account, and indicated they have met in real life.

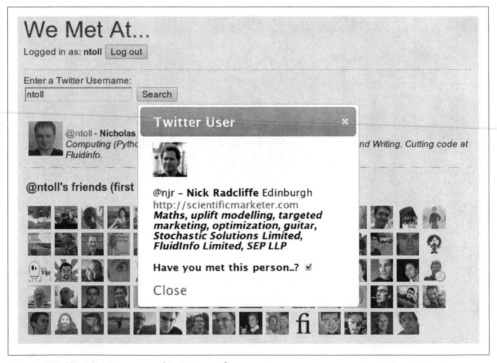

Figure 3-4. We Met At—created in just an afternoon

This simple application was created with just HTML and JavaScript, coded in a single afternoon, and demonstrates how quick and easy using Fluidinfo can be. It also shows how applications can piggyback upon and provide a service for emerging conventions observed within Fluidinfo (in this case the use of the met tag on objects about Twitter users).

Tunkrank: Adding Value to Twitter Data

Another source of Twitter-based data in Fluidinfo is Tunkrank (*http://tunkrank.com/*). It measures a person's influence on Twitter based upon how much attention her followers give her. Each user's attention is spread out among all the other users she follows. The more users she follows, the less attention they can give. Influence is expressed as a score reflecting how much attention a user's followers can give to her directly as well as how much attention they bring to the user from their own network of followers.

Tunkrank tags a user's score to the very same objects that Tickery and We Met At use (objects *about* Twitter users). In this way, the data from several sources begins to coalesce around shared openly writable objects.

Tunkrank's data is in Fluidinfo via tags in the tunkrank.com namespace. Simply by having such data *in* Fluidinfo, Tunkrank instantly gets a simple, searchable, and consistent RESTful API, and Fluidinfo users benefit from yet another interesting yet hard-to-gather dimension of information.

A Query Like No Other

These examples demonstrate three important things about Fluidinfo:

Fluidinfo is openly writable
> Tickery didn't have to ask for permission to annotate objects about Twitter users' influence.

Conventions emerge
> We Met At didn't have to use the met tag to indicate users had met someone in real life, but since many people were already doing so, it's an obvious thing to copy. Conventions such as this are emerging and evolving all the time in Fluidinfo (and more will be mentioned in this book).

There is no restriction on which tags to use in a query
> You need only to have read permission on a tag to be able to use it in a query. This makes it easy to search for things using information from different sources in a way that the owners of the tags may not have foreseen.

This last point is illustrated by the query shown below. It finds all the people Terry follows on Twitter that Terry hasn't met and that appear to be influential according to Tunkrank. Try typing the query into Tickery in *advanced* mode (the result of which can be seen in Figure 3-5):

```
(
    has twitter.com/friends/terrycojones
    and tunkrank.com/score > 25
)
except has terrycojones/met
```

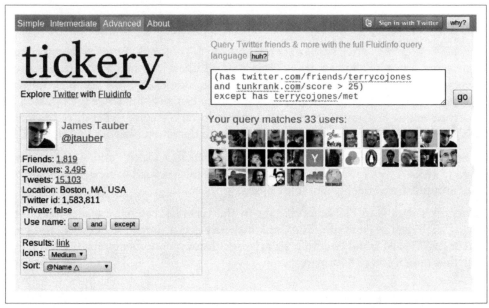

Figure 3-5. Tickery's advanced mode displaying the results of a query that references tags from different sources

O'Reilly Metadata

Now we'll turn to another dataset on Twitter, one that allows anyone to comment on a book and see other's comments. This was facilitated by a project at O'Reilly Media to load metadata about its books onto Fluidinfo, but it could be done for any dataset as long as people are willing to upload the information.

Instant API

As has already been observed, an important side effect of creating *social* data in Fluidinfo is that it instantly gets a simple, powerful, and *consistent* API[7] that includes functionality for search and contributions from third parties. A good example of this phenomenon is represented by all of the metadata from O'Reilly.

---

7. An API is an application programming interface: a mechanism for interacting with an application (in this case Fluidinfo).

As with the Twitter data, the O'Reilly data is represented straightforwardly. Two types of object are annotated: those representing products (usually books) and those representing the creators of products (usually authors). These objects are annotated with tags in the `oreilly.com` namespace.

Within the `oreilly.com` namespace are a set of *top-level* tags used to describe products in the O'Reilly catalog (for example, the `title`, `summary`, and URL tags). In addition, there are two *child* namespaces in the `oreilly.com` namespace: `authors` (containing tags to annotate information about an author) and `media` (containing a list of tags to indicate the type of product an object represents).

The simplicity of Fluidinfo (values tagged to objects) limits the potential for the originator of the data to create a complex schema. This was done on purpose, because data can be social only if it is easy to parse and understand.

Using the API

Interaction with the API is via simple HTTP requests that usually return easy-to-read JSON[8] objects. For example, making a request to

```
http://fluiddb.fluidinfo.com/objects?query=oreilly.com/title matches "Python"
```

returns a list of the IDs of objects that have "Python" in their titles. The JSON result looks something like this:

```
{
  ids: [
    "40bd2787-9010-4206-b988-ec3c284b647c",
    "f340b23b-8551-4c78-91e0-afe60c4cad52",
    "d59cfce8-b812-49bb-9adc-09cd89d1f13a",
    "1a91e021-7bce-4693-bfa5-0dc437fe1817",
    "0da922fe-6e0b-4982-8110-d24f5ebc77c9",
    "1d25baae-b977-4ff4-bb77-01c52bd1d339",
    "3360f05f-9bf4-4da5-abc0-0e3742809b98",
    "9845b184-ef1b-46fb-8e7c-011da053dcb6",
    "cd0838db-96ae-42ae-98c9-248a1507e2bb",
    "1b9dea59-c40a-462c-868a-4c43796417e9",
    "01371c03-9097-4267-a137-ae88a23790ef",
    "4bb7b433-b8d4-4a06-a3c6-460445217355",
    "4e9c42b6-68cb-43f5-9b75-60af9c0bd5a7",
    "4310538e-0a15-4b8a-9859-88ddb8833f93",
    "5bdb8134-1189-4fd9-ace9-4c32c90f0044",
    "527e153f-1b5c-4ade-8d6d-3c45d3e18501"
  ]
}
```

You don't need to be a developer to understand that the raw result is a list of IDs. Also, notice that exactly the same query language as that used in Tickery's advanced mode is used to write the query. It's simply appended to the URL as the `query` argument.

---

8. JavaScript Object Notation (*http://json.org*)

To return more interesting results from a search, simply append the list of tags whose values you are interested in to the end of the URL. For example, to find the title, authors, and publication year of all O'Reilly titles that have "Python" in their titles, make a request to

```
http://fluiddb.fluidinfo.com/objects?query=oreilly.com/title matches
"Python"&tag=oreilly.com/title&tag=oreilly.com/author-names&
tag=oreilly.com/publication-year
```

A fragment of the result is shown below:

```
{
  results: {
    id: {
      9845b184-ef1b-46fb-8e7c-011da053dcb6: {
        oreilly.com/title: {
          value: "Python Programming On Win32"
        },
        oreilly.com/author-names: {
          value: [
            "Mark Hammond",
            "Andy Robinson"
          ]
        },
        oreilly.com/publication-year: {
          value: 2000
        }
      },
      0da922fe-6e0b-4982-8110-d24f5ebc77c9: {
        oreilly.com/title: {
          value: "Programming Python, Third Edition"
        },
        oreilly.com/author-names: {
          value: [
            "Mark Lutz"
          ]
        },
        oreilly.com/publication-year: {
          value: 2006
        }
      },

      ... more results (truncated) ...
    }
  }
}
```

It's left as an exercise for the reader to figure out what the snippet of JSON above shows. (One of the great strengths of JSON is that it is easy for both humans and computers to read.)

Another interesting API query is to ask for all of the tags on a specific object. To do that, simply make sure the object's ID is in the path of the URL:

```
http://fluiddb.fluidinfo.com/objects/0da922fe-6e0b-4982-8110-d24f5ebc77c9
```

The result is a list of all of the tags on the object that you have permission to read.[9]

```
{
  tagPaths: [
    "fluiddb/about",
    "oreilly.com/publication-date",
    "amazon/sales-rank",
    "amazon/height",
    "librarything/url",
    "njr/index/about",
    "oreilly.com/id",
    "oreilly.com/publication-day",
    "amazon/asin",
    "amazon/weight",
    "amazon/price/gbp",
    "davidk01/amazon.com/suggestions",
    "amazon/url",
    "googlebooks/url",
    "oreilly.com/homepage",
    "goodreads/url",
    "oreilly.com/isbn",
    "goodreads/id",
    "amazon/price/usd",
    "oreilly.com/description",
    "orcilly.com/publication-year",
    "amazon/dewey-decimal",
    "amazon/width"
  ]
}
```

This example illustrates how the openly writable nature of social data encourages contributions from many people. Because a tag's name is qualified by its namespace path, one can work out what sort of data is attached to the object and by whom. O'Reilly may have initially created the object (which they don't own, because objects are openly writable entities that can never be deleted), but others have annotated it with all sorts of useful information, some of which O'Reilly might find useful.

The provision of a simple API over any data added to Fluidinfo is immensely useful and valuable. But it is the openly writable and *social* nature of Fluidinfo that is unique and that we'll explore in the following O'Reilly-related examples.

Skillshelves: Repurposing and Augmenting O'Reilly Data

Skillshelves (*http://www.skillshelv.es*) is an independent third-party application created by Jonas Neubert (*http://www.jonasneubert.com*) to estimate a user's level of skill in various technical areas based upon their O'Reilly reading habits.

---

9. Data from Amazon, Google Books, and other similar services has been imported into Fluidinfo for demonstration purposes. The amazon.com namespace isn't used because it's reserved for the owner of that domain.

Very little of the data used by the Skillshelves application is sourced by the author. Practically all of it is derived from data supplied by O'Reilly. However, many of the O'Reilly books have two types of tags under the `skillshelves` namespace. One indicates the difficulty of a work in relation to a particular skill, and the other indicates ownership.

For example, the object about the O'Reilly book *Natural Language Processing with Python* has a `skillshelves/skills/Python` tag with the associated value 30. It also has several `skillshelves/user/USERNAME` tags.

Since O'Reilly doesn't provide any categorization of its books by skill level, this addition to Fluidinfo by Skillshelves is useful. Of course, it depends on users trusting the rating information provided by Skillshelves. They can be sure that the information must have come from Skillshelves, since it's tagged from within the `skillshelves` top-level namespace. The provenance of the data is secure.

From a practical point of view, it's possible to see how this data is mashed up by visiting the Skillshelves website itself. Figure 3-6 shows an example bookshelf along with a display of Skillshelves' assessment of the reader's profile.

A Query Like No Other

Given such a profusion of data surrounding O'Reilly-related objects, it's relatively simple to construct Fluidinfo queries that combine tags from all sorts of seemingly unrelated sources. For example, what are the easy titles about Python that don't weigh too much (suitable as a pocket book for beginning Python programmers)?

```
oreilly.com/title matches "Python"
and skillshelves/skills/Python="10"
and amazon/weight<200
```

Blog Mining and Emerging Conventions

Blogs, by their very nature, are social enterprises: authors publish articles and people on the Internet respond with comments. Unfortunately, it is often hard to explore blogs because they're arranged in a linear fashion, store their data in hidden databases, have no API, and often organize themselves only through simple tagging and similar categorizations of articles. Fluidinfo has been applied to this area as well.

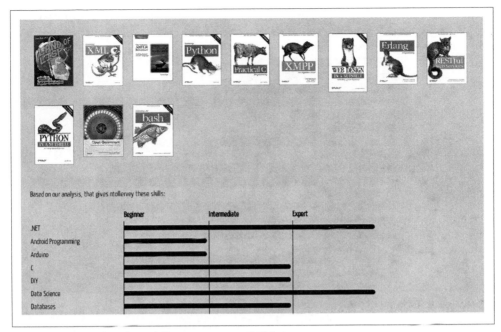

Figure 3-6. Using data from different sources in Skillshelves

Boing Boing

Boing Boing (*http://boingboing.net*) is a long-running culture/technology blog that has released all its articles from the past 11 years as an XML dump covered by a Creative Commons license. The XML was parsed and imported into Fluidinfo—turning a verbose splurge of markup (see Example 3-1) into a searchable database of articles.

Example 3-1. Unfriendly XML representing a Boing Boing article

```
<row>
    <permalink>http://boingboing.net/2000/01/21/street-tech-reviews-.html</permalink>
    <created_on>2000-01-21 14:07:38</created_on>
    <basename>street_tech_reviews_</basename>
    <author>Mark Frauenfelder</author>
    <title>Street Tech Reviews and news</title>
    <body><
A HREF="http://www.streettech.com/">Street Tech</A>
Reviews and news for gadget-lovers and propeller heads of all stripes.
    </body>
    <body_more>NULL</body_more>
    <comment_count>0</comment_count>
    <categories>NULL</categories>
</row>
```

Every article and author in Boing Boing's data dump is represented by an object in Fluidinfo. Figure 3-7 is a representation of a typical object about a Boing Boing article.

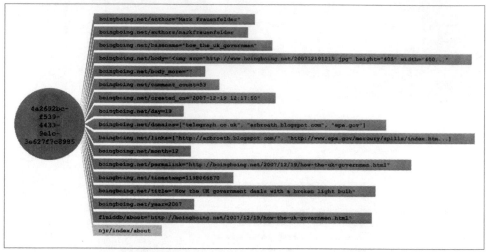

Figure 3-7. A Boing Boing article in Fluidinfo

The original names of the XML tags used to mark up the data formed the basis of the tag names created in Fluidinfo underneath the `boingboing.net` namespace.

When the original XML data was parsed, every domain name and URL referenced in each article was extracted and all the dates were translated into computer-friendly values. The data derived from this process was also added to Boing Boing–related objects. Furthermore, every domain mentioned in a Boing Boing article has an object in Fluidinfo with *a list of Boing Boing articles that reference the domain* tagged to it. For example, there's an object *about* the `bbc.co.uk` domain with an associated list of Boing Boing articles attached to it.

ReadWriteWeb

ReadWriteWeb (*http://www.readwriteweb.com/*) is another technology-related blog that focuses on web technology and news. Its back catalog of the almost 11,300 articles written since 2003 is available in Fluidinfo, and ReadWriteWeb's data is also represented as a set of tagged objects for each article and author. The tags can be found in the `readwriteweb.com` namespace.

Another similarity with the Boing Boing data is that as each article was parsed, all the domains and URLs were extracted. Furthermore, each domain mentioned was tagged with a list of ReadWriteWeb articles that reference the domain in exactly the same way as with the Boing Boing data.

The important point is that *conventions apply to more than just the names of tags* (as in the example of the *met* tag co-opted by the We Met At application). Conventions can apply to behavior: in this case, an expectation that domains will be extracted from blog content and annotated with lists of articles that mention them.

The Boing Boing and ReadWriteWeb tags are similar but *not the same*. The *scheme* of the original data is retained but both datasets coalesce around objects *about* domains. In this way the imported data is following social norms and conventions with regard to referenced domains. Yet another way data can be said to be *social*.

Union Square Ventures

Union Square Ventures (*http://www.usv.com/*) is a well-known venture capital fund that invests in technology startups. Its website is, among other things, a blog containing articles from the partners and it contains a list of the company's investments. This list was imported into Fluidinfo by founder Terry Jones as an exercise in creating a minimal viable way to publish data.[10]

The API is built on a very simple scheme: attach a `unionsquareventures.com/portfolio` tag to objects *about* the domains of companies in Union Square Ventures' portfolio.

Notice the reuse of the convention of tagging domains.

A Query Like No Other

It is possible to extract information unavailable anywhere else about blogs simply because the data described earlier makes use of the behavioral convention of tagging domains. Furthermore, at no point in the import process did any of the originators of the data expect to be able to make the following query:

```
has boingboing.net/mentioned
and has readwriteweb.com/mentioned
and has unionsquareventures.com/portfolio
```

This query finds all companies backed by Union Square Ventures that have been mentioned in articles on both Boing Boing and ReadWriteWeb. If the `fluiddb/about` tag is selected to be returned, the objects the query returns are the following:

- `twitter.com`
- `etsy.com`
- `boxee.tv`
- `meetup.com`

It is also possible for Fluidinfo to return the list of referencing articles (stored in the `boingboing.net/mentioned` and `readwriteweb.com/mentioned` tags). The result for `meetup.com` looks like this:

---

10. Terry explains what he did on the Fluidinfo blog (*http://blogs.fluidinfo.com/fluidinfo/2011/02/15/how-i-made-a-writable-api-for-union-square-ventures-in-an-hour/*).

```
{
    "boingboing.net/mentioned":
      {"value": [
        "http://boingboing.net/2009/11/06/vampireotherkinenerg.html",
        "http://boingboing.net/2010/01/11/ny-times-on-urban-ca.html",
        "http://boingboing.net/2010/10/26/ron-paul-supporter-w.html",
        "http://boingboing.net/2002/06/27/meetup-meatspace-cam.html",
        "http://boingboing.net/2004/03/17/wired-rave-awards.html",
        "http://boingboing.net/2006/01/05/net-pug-nabbed-by-cr.html"]
      },
    "fluiddb/about": {"value": "meetup.com"},
    "readwriteweb.com/mentioned":
      {"value": [
        "http://www.readwriteweb.com/archives/meetup_the_secret_campaign_weapon.php"
        ]
      }
}
```

Social Data

In this chapter we have tried to show what it means, concretely, for data to be social and writable, and how Fluidinfo supports these ideas with a simple, powerful, and consistent API. A key theme is that data can be reused (subject to permissions), by anyone, for purposes that might have been entirely unanticipated by the initial data provider. Another is that because *all objects* are shared in Fluidinfo, anyone can store information about anything, and, subject to conventions, relevant data will naturally coalesce. This creates increasing opportunities for mashups and other forms of reuse within and around Fluidinfo.

With this in mind, the following chapters explore how to make use of Fluidinfo in programs of your own.

CHAPTER 4

Programming with Fluidinfo

Client Libraries

The easiest way to make use of Fluidinfo in your own programming projects is to use an existing client library. There are many open source libraries available in many different languages. A comprehensive list can be found on Fluidinfo's developer page (*http://fluidinfo.com/about/fluidinfo%20for%20developers/developers*). Such client libraries can be categorized in two ways:

- Asynchronous versus synchronous clients[1]
- Thin layers just above the HTTP API versus programmer-friendly abstractions (for example, an object-oriented mapping to Fluidinfo)

This chapter and the two that follow introduce three libraries that illustrate the categories described above:

fluidinfo.py
> A blocking client that provides a bare-minimum client library for Fluidinfo's HTTP API (presented in this chapter)

FOM (the Fluid Object Mapper)
> A blocking, object-oriented abstraction for using Fluidinfo (presented in Chapter 5)

fluidinfo.js
> An asynchronous library that provides both low-level interactions with the API and high-level functions that abstract common tasks (presented in Chapter 6)

---

1. Asynchronous clients make a request to Fluidinfo, continue with what they're doing, and associate a piece of code to handle the response when it arrives (these are usually known as callbacks). In contrast, synchronous clients are said to *block*: when they make a call to Fluidinfo the program waits for a response before continuing.

Although there is a danger that programs built upon synchronous libraries can become unresponsive while they wait for responses from Fluidinfo,[2] it does mean that the code written with these libraries is easy to read and understand.

Alternatively, if you'd like to use the API directly, you should refer to Chapter 7, which explains and illustrates the raw HTTP-based API in detail.

Introducing fluidinfo.py

The *fluidinfo.py (https://github.com/fluidinfo/fluidinfo.py)* library is a very thin wrapper around Fluidinfo's HTTP-based API. It provides just enough functionality that you don't have to worry about how your interaction with Fluidinfo happens. You only need to understand the API and make obvious calls to it via the `fluidinfo` module.

fluidinfo.py requires Python 2.6 (*http://python.org/*) (or later) to work, so we assume you have followed the instructions at the Python website (*http://python.org/down load/*) to install an appropriate version on your system. With this requirement met, there are two platform-independent ways to install the library:

- Use Python's own installation tools: *easy_install* or *pip*.
- Install from the source code.

The first option assumes you have Python's *setuptools (http://pypi.python.org/pypi/se tuptools)* or *pip (http://www.pip-installer.org/)* installed. With one of these, you should be able to install *fluidinfo.py* by typing commands similar to the following into your terminal:

```
$ easy_install fluidinfo.py
$ pip install -U fluidinfo.py
```

If all goes well, some messages will scroll down the screen that end with an indication that the package is installed.

Alternatively, download the source code from the project's website and use the *setup.py* installation script.

The *fluidinfo.py* source code is freely available (*https://github.com/fluidinfo/fluidinfo .py*) and there's an obvious link to download the code as a compressed file (which you should uncompress to somewhere on your file system). Alternatively, use the Git (*http: //git-scm.com/*) source control tool to track the project repository on your local file system.

In either case you'll end up with a directory containing the source code. Change into the directory and install *fluidinfo.py* by typing the following command into your shell:

```
$ python setup.py install
```

---

2. A problem that can easily be overcome through sensible use of threading or other programming mechanisms.

(You may need some sort of administrative privileges for this to work.)

To check everything works, simply start a Python session and type in the following:

```
$ python
Python 2.6.5 (r265:79063, Apr 16 2010, 13:09:56)
[GCC 4.4.3] on linux2
Type "help", "copyright", "credits" or "license" for more information.
>>> import fluidinfo
>>> exit()
```

If you get an "ImportError" message, it's likely that the library isn't in your Python path. Check the Python documentation for more information about how to set the path correctly.

Fluidinfo.py Fundamentals

The primary goals of *fluidinfo.py* are simplicity, ease of use, and the principle of least surprise. Ultimately, if you know the HTTP API (*http://api.fluidinfo.com/*), it should be obvious what to do with this library. The following example from an interactive Python session illustrates this:

```
>>> import fluidinfo ❶
>>> fluidinfo.login('username', 'password') ❷
>>> fluidinfo.get('/users/alice') ❸
({ 'status': '200',
   'content-length': '71',
   'content-location': 'https://fluiddb.fluidinfo.com/users/alice',
   'server': 'nginx/0.7.65',
   'connection': 'keep-alive',
   'cache-control': 'no-cache',
   'date': 'Thu, 14 Jul 2011 12:36:29 GMT',
   'content-type': 'application/json'},
 { u'name': u'Alice Liddell',
   u'id': u'1494b708-0665-4608-9366-e3c161ef313c'}
)
```

❶   Import the fluidinfo library into the Python session.

❷   Log in, passing in your username as the first argument followed by your pass-
     word. It's a good idea *never* to hardcode a password into code.

❸   Make an HTTP GET request to the /users/alice endpoint.

The example shows how to get information about the user alice. The result consists of two dictionaries—the HTTP response headers and the JSON payload returned by Fluidinfo. Notice how *fluidinfo.py* takes care of authentication and silently translates the raw JSON response from Fluidinfo into a native Python dictionary.

There are functions for each of the HTTP methods[3] used with the HTTP API. For example, creating a new object involves sending an HTTP POST request to the / objects endpoint with a JSON specification of the *about* value. As the following example shows, simply call the post function with the appropriate arguments (a single JSON payload describing the new object):

```
>>> payload = {'about': 'wonderland'}
>>> headers, response = fluidinfo.post('/objects', payload)
>>> headers
{'status': '201',
 'content-length': '131',
 'server': 'nginx/0.7.65',
 'connection': 'keep-alive',
 'location': 'https://fluiddb.fluidinfo.com/objects/1f296e02-6e5a-41e0-
acb8-145d8063c549',
 'cache-control': 'no-cache',
 'date': 'Wed, 13 Jul 2011 14:08:13 GMT',
 'content-type': 'application/json'}
>>> response
{u'id': u'1f296e02-6e5a-41e0-acb8-145d8063c549',
 u'URI': u'https://fluiddb.fluidinfo.com/objects/1f296e02-6e5a-41e0-
acb8-145d8063c549'}
```

Notice how *fluidinfo.py* has silently translated the native Python dictionary (containing the definition of what the new object is about) into the JSON payload. Furthermore, the Python tuple returned by *fluidinfo.py* is assigned to two variables representing the headers and response.

Tagging an object requires a single HTTP PUT request and retrieving a tag value is a single GET request:

```
>>> headers, response = fluidinfo.put('/about/wonderland/alice/rating', 11) ❶
>>> headers, response = fluidinfo.get('/about/wonderland/alice/rating') ❷
>>> response
11
```

❶ Add/update the integer value 11 to the object about "wonderland" via the alice/ rating tag.

❷ Return the value of the tag.

The simple pattern for creating a request with *fluidinfo.py* is to call a function named after the HTTP method, with the path to the desired endpoint and (optional) value to upload as the two arguments:

```
fluidinfo.METHOD('/PATH/TO/ENDPOINT', VALUE)
```

Some calls, following Fluidinfo's HTTP API, require additional arguments. For example, when retrieving values from objects that match a particular query, you need to supply both the list of tags whose values you want to retrieve and the query itself (the equivalent of a SELECT/WHERE statement in SQL):

---

3. GET, POST, PUT, DELETE, and HEAD.

```
>>> tag_list = ['fluiddb/about', 'alice/rating', 'oreilly.com/title']
>>> query_to_match = 'oreilly.com/title matches "Python"'
>>> headers, result = fluidinfo.get('/values', tags=tag_list,
...     query=query_to_match)
```

At a low level there needs to be an HTTP GET call to the **/values** endpoint. However, the HTTP API needs appropriately URL-encoded arguments for the tag list and query. Happily, *fluidinfo.py* does the heavy lifting and makes the appropriate translation from the arguments passed into the Python function to those needed by the Fluidinfo API.

Another similar requirement is to append arguments to an endpoint to tell Fluidinfo how much information you want returned. For example, when getting information about a namespace, you can optionally ask for its description, child namespaces, and tags. The Fluidinfo API states that these should be passed as arguments in the URL, so *fluidinfo.py* helps by turning any arguments you pass (in addition to the endpoint and value) into URL arguments:

```
>>> fluidinfo.get('/namespaces/boingboing.net',
... returnDescription=True, returnNamespaces=True, returnTags=True)
```

The result is a GET request to the following URL:

```
https://fluiddb.fluidinfo.com/namespaces/boingboing.net?returnDescription=True&
returnNamespaces=True&returnTags=True
```

Common Tasks Using fluidinfo.py

The *fluidinfo.py* library makes it very easy to explore Fluidinfo's API in an interactive Python session. What follows is a list of basic tasks users most often want to do with the Fluidinfo API along with examples of how to make them work using *fluidinfo.py*. A growing list of such "recipes" can be found on Fluidinfo's cookbook (*http://fluidinfo .com/cookbook*) page.

Create a New Object

There are two ways to create a new object:

1. HTTP POST to the **/objects** endpoint to create objects that may or may not have an associated *about* value.
2. HTTP POST to the **/about** endpoint.

The following session demonstrates how to use the **/about** endpoint:

```
>>> headers, response = fluidinfo.post('/about/terry jones')
>>> headers
{'cache-control': 'no-cache',
 'connection': 'keep-alive',
 'content-length': '131',
 'content-type': 'application/json',
 'date': 'Tue, 29 Aug 2011 11:52:16 GMT',
 'location': 'https://fluiddb.fluidinfo.com/about/terry%20jones',
```

```
 'server': 'nginx/0.7.65',
 'status': '201'}
>>> response
{u'URI': u'https://fluiddb.fluidinfo.com/about/terry%20jones',
 u'id': u'79a9a9ed-15cd-4357-a434-f9b322ff8074'}
```

Notice how Fluidinfo responds with the canonical URI for the object along with its unique ID. The 201 status in the headers indicates that the operation succeeded. If there is already an object about "terry jones", the call returns details of the existing object (in other words, no new object is created).

Tag an Object with a Value

As with the creation of objects, it is possible to use both the /objects and /about endpoints for manipulating values tagged on objects. The following examples use the /about endpoint, because using an "about" value makes them easier to understand.

Two types of value can be stored in Fluidinfo. Primitive values can be used in search queries and include numbers, Boolean values, strings, and lists of strings. Opaque values include any other type of data with an associated MIME type and cannot be used in a search query.

 A MIME type (Multipurpose Internet Mail Extension) is a two-part identifier for file formats. Originally developed to allow non-ASCII multimedia content in mail messages, its most common use now is perhaps as the value that's passed via the content-type header in HTTP. Its purpose is to indicate the *type* of data being transmitted. For example, the MIME type for a PNG image is image/png (notice the two-part *type/subtype* distinction). In the context of Fluidinfo, you *must* indicate a MIME type for all opaque values. When the value is subsequently retrieved, Fluidinfo adds the appropriate content-type header to the response. (Fluidinfo uses the MIME type application/vnd.fluiddb.value +json to indicate simple tag values.)

Remember, to tag an object with a primitive value, simply pass the correct endpoint path (consisting of the object's about value with the tag's path appended to the end) and the actual Python value to the put function. The library takes care of the rest:

```
>>> headers, response = fluidinfo.put('/about/fluidinfo/alice/rating', 10)
>>> headers
{'cache-control': 'no-cache',
 'connection': 'keep-alive',
 'content-type': 'text/html',
 'date': 'Tue, 29 Aug 2011 20:13:25 GMT',
 'server': 'nginx/0.7.65',
 'status': '204'}
```

The 204 status code in the headers indicates the operation succeeded.

Tagging an opaque value works in exactly the same way but with the addition of a mime argument:

```
>>> headers, response = fluidinfo.put('/about/fluidinfo/alice/comment',
... '<html><body><h1>Fluidinfo</h1><p>An interesting project.</p></body></html>',
... mime='text/html')
```

Notice that we are declaring the text to have the MIME type text/html, rather than letting the library convert it to Fluidinfo's primitive string type. To store a binary value, such as an image, you might do something like this:

```
>>> kittyImage = open('kitten.png')
>>> headers, response = fluidinfo.put('/about/fluidinfo/alice/kitten',
... kittyImage.read(), mime='image/png')
```

Get a Specific Value from an Object

To retrieve individual values from an object, simply send an HTTP GET request to the appropriate path:

```
>>> headers, response = fluidinfo.get('/about/fluidinfo/alice/rating')
>>> headers
{'cache-control': 'no-cache',
 'connection': 'keep-alive',
 'content-length': '2',
 'content-location': 'https://fluiddb.fluidinfo.com/about/fluidinfo/alice/rating',
 'content-type': 'application/vnd.fluiddb.value+json',
 'date': 'Tue, 29 Aug 2011 21:26:12 GMT',
 'server': 'nginx/0.7.65',
 'status': '200'}
>>> response
10
```

This example returns the value of the alice/rating tag on the object about fluidinfo.

Notice that the library has converted the response into a Python integer type. It knows to do this because the content-type header has the value application/vnd.fluiddb.value+json. This is the MIME type used by Fluidinfo to indicate that the payload of a response or request is a primitive type. If the value being returned was an opaque value, the content-header would reflect this. For example, if an image were being returned, the content-header would be something like image/png.

Delete a Specific Value from an Object

Deleting a specific value from an object requires that you make an HTTP DELETE request to an endpoint that references the object and affected tag:

```
>>> headers, response = fluidinfo.delete('/about/fluidinfo/alice/rating')
>>> headers
{'cache-control': 'no-cache',
 'connection': 'keep-alive',
 'content-type': 'text/html',
 'date': 'Tue, 29 Aug 2011 21:37:21 GMT',
```

```
'server': 'nginx/0.7.65',
'status': '204'}
```

This example deletes the value associated with the `alice/rating` tag from the object about `fluidinfo`.

The status header's 204 value informs us that the tag/value was deleted. Fluidinfo doesn't return anything in the response.

Query for Specified Values on Matching Objects

Queries are specified with the language described in the Appendix. By specifying one or more tags it is possible to build a request that is the equivalent to the following SQL-like query:

```
SELECT tag1, tag2, tag3 FROM fluidinfo WHERE query=…
```

This is achieved with a GET request to a **/values**-based URL that has, in addition to the query argument, a list of the tags whose values should be returned:

```
>>> headers, response = fluidinfo.get('/values',
... tags=['alice/rating', 'alice/comment', 'alice/kitten'],
... query='has alice/rating')
>>> response
{u'results':
  {u'id':
    {u'0ff5ba6a-b901-41c6-ab76-516183379e41':
      {u'alice/rating': {u'value': 10}},
     u'2eecb420-9a1f-497b-9654-c07dd86fa926':
      {u'alice/rating': {u'value': 5},
       u'alice/comment': {u'value': u'It was ok'},
       u'alice/kitten': {u'size': 3952, u'value-type': u'image/png'}
      }
    }
  }
}
```

This example requests the values of the `alice/rating`, `alice/comment`, and `alice/kit ten` tags on all objects that have been tagged with the `alice/rating` tag. The result is a Python dictionary created from the raw JSON that Fluidinfo responded with.

It is important to note the following about the result:

* Each matching object is referenced by its object ID.
* No value component is returned if the matching object doesn't have a selected tag (see the first result, which has no `alice/comment` or `alice/kitten` values).
* If the value is a primitive type, it will be returned inline (see the results for the `alice/rating` and `alice/comment` tags).
* If the value is an opaque type, its size and MIME type will be returned (see the result for the `alice/kitten` tag). In order to get the actual value, you should GET

the individual tag as described in "Get a Specific Value from an Object" on page 49.

Armed with these examples and a specification of the Fluidinfo HTTP API (*http://api .fluidinfo.com/*), it is a relatively simple exercise to build quite complex requests with the minimum of effort. However, such interactions can sometimes feel clumsy, because the RESTful nature of Fluidinfo's API may not fit with the programming paradigm being used in your application. These problems are addressed by more abstract libraries such as FOM, which we'll explore in the next chapter.

CHAPTER 5

Programming with FOM

The Fluid Object Mapper (*https://launchpad.net/fom*) (FOM) serves the same purpose as an Object Relational Mapper (ORM) in the context of traditional relational databases. In other words, it provides object-oriented access to Fluidinfo.

In contrast to the lower-level *fluidinfo.py*, FOM is quick and convenient, hiding many of the implementation details from the developer. However, it is similar to *fluidinfo.py* in that it is a synchronous library—it pauses program execution while it waits for responses from Fluidinfo.

Like *fluidinfo.py*, FOM requires Python 2.6 (*http://python.org/*) (or later) to work and can be installed using exactly the same tools and techniques described for *fluidinfo.py*:

```
$ easy_install fom
$ pip install -U fom
```

Furthermore, the source code is hosted online (*http://launchpad.net/fom*) and you should be able to download it or clone the project using the `bzr` source control tool. Once you have the source, you can install FOM by changing into the source directory and typing the following command into your shell:

```
$ python setup.py install
```

(You may need some sort of administrative privileges for this to work.)

FOM Fundamentals

FOM is to Fluidinfo as an ORM is to a relational database. It's built of two layers:

1. A low-level thin wrapper for the actual REST API, which has functionality similar to the *fluidinfo.py* library.
2. An object-oriented layer built on the low-level API.

FOM binds to a session. You can optionally log in to a session or you can remain anonymous. The following Python shell-based example illustrates basic use of FOM:

```
>>> from fom.session import Fluid ❶
>>> session = Fluid()
>>> session.login('alice', 'password') ❷
>>> session.bind() ❸
>>> from fom.mapping import Object
>>> o = Object(about="wonderland") ❹
>>> o.tag_paths ❺
[u'alice/rating', u'fluiddb/about', ... truncated list of tag paths ...]
>>> session.logout()❻
```

❶ The `Fluid` class in FOM's `fom.session` module looks after sessions.

❷ Log in can happen at any time and on many occasions during the life of a session.

❸ Calling `bind()` sets everything up. If you miss this step, nothing will work.

❹ Instantiate a `fom.mapping.Object` class that maps to the *object in Fluidinfo* that represents "wonderland" (its *about* value is "wonderland").

❺ Objects have lots of useful methods and attributes. This one lists all the tags attached to the referenced object.

❻ It is important to note that the session is still active but any subsequent calls would be made as the anonymous user.

All the classes representing abstractions used by Fluidinfo can be found in the `fom.mapping` module. The rest of this chapter will introduce these abstractions and end with a simple example script that imports data into Fluidinfo.

Namespaces and Tags

As we explained in earlier chapters, *tags* attach data to objects. *Namespaces* organize and categorize tags in some meaningful way. *Permissions* apply to both tags and namespaces. These are the primary means of structuring and controlling access to data within Fluidinfo. This section shows how to use FOM to create, update, and delete some namespaces and tags (permissions are dealt with later).

Within the `fom.mapping` module there are two classes, called `Namespace` and `Tag`. Instances of these classes map to specific namespaces and tags within Fluidinfo.

Every user has a top-level namespace that has the same name as his or her username. Therefore, the user `alice` has a top-level namespace that is also called `alice`. It is in these top-level namespaces that users create the namespace and tag structure used to represent the data being stored in Fluidinfo.

To create an instance of either the `Namespace` or `Tag` classes, simply pass in the correct path when instantiating it:

```
>>> from fom.mapping import Namespace, Tag
>>> aliceNamespace = Namespace('alice')
>>> aliceRatingTag = Tag('alice/rating')
```

These objects have some useful methods and attributes that hide and encapsulate the HTTP calls going on under the hood. For example, every namespace and tag has an associated description that is exposed as the `description` attribute:

```
>>> aliceNamespace.description
u'Namespace for user alice'
>>> aliceNamespace.description = "Alice's namespace"
>>> aliceNamespace.description
u"Alice's namespace"
```

Since `description` is an attribute, getting and setting the value silently causes FOM to make the appropriate updates to Fluidinfo. `Namespace` objects have two more useful attributes to get the child tags and namespaces contained within the instantiated namespace:

```
>>> aliceNamespace.tag_paths
[u'alice/rating', u'alice/has-read', u'alice/comment', u'alice/favourite-things'
, u'alice/to-read']
>>> aliceNamespace.namespace_paths
[u'alice/private', u'alice/alice', u'alice/test-fish']
```

A more useful alternative is to get a list of appropriately instantiated child tags and namespaces:

```
>>> aliceNamespace.tags
[<Tag path=u'alice/rating'>, <Tag path=u'alice/has-read'>,
<Tag path=u'alice/comment'>, <Tag path=u'alice/favourite-things'>,
<Tag path=u'alice/to-read'>]
>>> aliceNamespace.namespaces
[<Namespace path=u'alice/private'>, <Namespace path=u'alice/alice'>,
<Namespace path=u'alice/test-fish'>]
```

Tags and namespaces are created *on first use*. However, if you want to explicitly create a namespace/tag structure, there are two helpful methods: `create_namespace` and `create_tag`. Both take the same two arguments: the name of the new namespace or tag and its description:

```
>>> bookNamespace = aliceNamespace.create_namespace('books', 'Tags about books') ❶
>>> titleTag = bookNamespace.create_tag('title', 'The title of a book') ❷
```

❶   Creates a new child namespace called `books`. A new namespace object representing the newly created namespace is returned.

❷   Creates a new tag called `title` under the `alice/books` namespace. A new Tag object is returned.

Sometimes a tag or namespace is no longer needed. In this case, both Tag and Namespace objects have a `delete` method that deletes the related tag or namespace in Fluidinfo.

It's important to note that it's only possible to delete empty namespaces (so all child namespaces and tags must be deleted first).

```
>>> bookNamespace.delete() ❶
Traceback (most recent call last):
... a stack trace ...
fom.errors.Fluid412Error: <TNamespaceNotEmpty (412 Precondition Failed)> ❷
>>> titleTag.delete() ❸
>>> bookNamespace.delete() ❹
<FluidResponse (204, 'text/html', None, '')>
```

❶❷ Calling the delete method on a nonempty namespace will result in a namespace not empty exception (Fluid412Error).

❸ Deleting the tag ensures the namespace is empty.

❹ Calling the delete method on the namespace produces a successful 204 HTTP response.

Working with Objects

Conventional ORM libraries often map a class definition to a table and an object instance to a specific row. The attributes of a class map in some way to the columns of the table, and getting and setting attribute values on an instance ultimately updates a row in the database somewhere.

Things are different (and simpler) in FOM. Fluidinfo objects represent things. Objects are usually about something specific (indicated by the fluiddb/about tag value). FOM maps Fluidinfo's objects to instances of classes that ultimately inherit from the Object class found in the fom.mapping module.

FOM's Object class provides a mechanism to work in an object-oriented way with Fluidinfo. Simply instantiating the Object class provides many helpful features:

```
>>> from fom.mapping import Object
>>> o = Object(about="wonderland") ❶
>>> o.tag_paths ❷
[u'musicbrainz.org/related-artists', u'wordtools/gcide',
u'wordtools/moby-thesaurus', u'fluiddb/about']
>>> o.tags ❸
[<Tag path=u'musicbrainz.org/related-artists'>,
<Tag path=u'wordtools/gcide'>, <Tag path=u'wordtools/moby-thesaurus'>,
<Tag path=u'fluiddb/about'>]
>>> o.get('wordtools/gcide') ❹
(u'Wonderland \\Won"der*land`\\, n.\nA land full of wonders, or marvels. --M.
Arnold.\n[1913 Webster]', 'application/vnd.fluiddb.value+json')
>>> o.set('alice/rating', 10) ❺
>>> o.tag_paths
[u'alice/rating', u'musicbrainz.org/related-artists', u'wordtools/gcide',
u'wordtools/moby-thesaurus', u'fluiddb/about']
>>> o.get('alice/rating')
(10, 'application/vnd.fluiddb.value+json')
>>> o.delete('alice/rating') ❻
>>> o.tag_paths
[u'musicbrainz.org/related-artists', u'wordtools/gcide',
u'wordtools/moby-thesaurus', u'fluiddb/about']
```

❶   Passing in the about argument indicates the object in Fluidinfo to map to the instantiated FOM object.

❷❸   Return a list of tag paths or instances of Tag objects that are attached to the referenced Fluidinfo object.

❹   Get the value associated with a Fluidinfo object via a specific tag with the get method. The result is a tuple containing the value followed by an indication of its MIME type (discussed below).

❺   Add or update a value with the set method. Pass in the tag path to use and the value to set.

❻   Remove a tag value from an object with the delete method.

Although these methods are useful, they're not always very convenient, because tags are exposed via methods rather than as an object's attributes. A far more elegant solution would be to associate tag values with attributes on an instance. This is very easy to achieve by using the fom.mapping.tag_value class to define attributes. Consider the following Python script (which we'll assume is called example.py for now):

```python
from fom.mapping import Object, tag_value


class Book(Object):
    """
    A class that defines how an object representing a book should look
    from Alice's perspective.
    """

    title = tag_value('alice/books/title')
    author = tag_value('alice/books/author')
    description = tag_value('alice/books/description')
    cover = tag_value('alice/books/cover', 'image/png')
    rating = tag_value('alice/books/rating')
```

Given this class definition, it's relatively simple to interact with Fluidinfo in an obvious and far more object-oriented way:

```python
>>> from example import Book
>>> wonderland = Book(about="alice's adventures in wonderland")
>>> wonderland.title = "Alice's Adventures in Wonderland"
>>> wonderland.author = "Lewis Carroll"
>>> wonderland.description = """Alice's Adventures in Wonderland (commonly
... shortened to Alice in Wonderland) is an 1865 novel written by English
... author Charles Lutwidge Dodgson under the pseudonym Lewis Carroll."""
>>> cover = open('aaiw.png', 'rb')
>>> wonderland.cover = cover.read()
>>> cover.close()
>>> wonderland.rating = 11
>>> wonderland.save()
```

FOM interacts with Fluidinfo in two places in this example. Since the cover attribute is a binary file (a PNG image), it is immediately added to Fluidinfo. This is because

Fluidinfo uses JSON to specify how to update multiple values on an object and JSON isn't a good way to send binary data. All the other values don't get added to Fluidinfo until **save** is called by default.

The **tag_value** class provides a couple of ways to define how values associated with the referenced tag are handled: the expected data type and when the value should be pushed to Fluidinfo.

Remember, Fluidinfo distinguishes between two types of tag value:

Primitive
> Numeric, Boolean, string, and list values that can be used by the query language

Opaque
> Any other value, identified by a MIME type (for example, **application/pdf**) and hidden from the query language

The **tag_value** class assumes primitive tag values by default. However, if you know that one of the referenced tags is supposed to hold some other sort of data, you can specify what this will be by passing a MIME type as the second argument when instantiating the **tag_value** class:

```
cover = tag_value('alice/books/cover', 'image/png')
```

It's also possible to specify when the **tag_value** object communicates with Fluidinfo. The defaults are sensible, but, if you need to change them, you can pass in two further arguments upon instantiation. Both are Boolean values whose default value is **True**:

cached
> If set to **False**, every time the value is retrieved via the object's attribute, an HTTP GET call is made to Fluidinfo.

lazy_save
> If set to **False**, every time a value is updated or assigned to the object's attribute, a call is made to Fluidinfo (rather than waiting for an explicit call to the object's **save** method).

Searching Objects

FOM wouldn't be very useful if it were not possible to search for interesting objects using the query language and retrieve associated tag values.

The **Object** class has a class method called **filter** (in other words, it is called on the class itself, not an instance thereof). The result is a list of Object instances that match the query:

```
>>> results = Object.filter('alice/rating=11 and has alice/books/title')
>>> len(results)
2
>>> results[0].about
u'through the looking-glass'
```

```
>>> results[1].about
u"alice's adventures in wonderland"
```

The problem with this approach is that only Object instances are returned. Getting and setting tag values on these instances is done on the fly, via methods rather than attributes, and such methods don't take advantage of FOM's caching capabilities. It is far better to ask for FOM to return prepopulated instances of classes that inherit from FOM's Object class (such as the Book class described earlier). This can be done in two ways:

- Calling the `filter` method on a subclass of the Object class. This will return prepopulated results that are instances of the subclass:

```
>>> from example import Book
>>> results = Book.filter('alice/rating=11 and has alice/books/title')
>>> len(results)
2
>>> results[0].title
u"Alice's Adventures in Wonderland"
>>> results[0].rating
11
>>> results[1].title
u'Through the Looking-Glass, and What Alice Found There'
>>> results[1].author
u'Lewis Carroll'
```

- Passing in the class you want to instantiate in the result set, using the `result_type` argument in a call to `filter` on the Object class:

```
>>> from example import Book
>>> results = Object.filter('alice/rating=11 and has alice/books/title',
...    result_type=Book)
>>> len(results)
2
>>> isinstance(results[0], Book)
True
```

Both methods produce the same result: a list of prepopulated instances that work in exactly the manner you would expect.

Working with Permissions

The only other major feature of Fluidinfo that FOM handles is permissions. To recap, permissions only apply to namespaces and tags, not to objects. Permissions are scoped by actions (such as `read`, `write`, `list`, and so on) and work in a similar way to black/white lists: each permission has an associated policy that is either open or closed and a list of exceptions to the policy.

For example, Alice may let only a select few people read her `alice/rating` tag. In fact, she lets her friend Bert read any values associated via the tag. To do this she sets the policy associated with the tag's `read` action as closed with an exceptions list containing her own and Bert's usernames.

FOM's `mapping` module contains a Permission class that can be used to express and manipulate this sort of information, as follows:

```
>>> from fom.mapping import Permission
>>> p = Permission('closed', ['alice', 'bert'])  ❶
>>> p
<Permission: closed except for ['alice', 'bert']>
>>> ratingTag = Tag('alice/rating')  ❷
>>> ratingTag.value_permissions['read']  ❸
<Permission: open except for []>
>>> ratingTag.value_permissions['read'] = p  ❹
>>> ratingTag.value_permissions['read']
<Permission: closed except for [u'bert', u'alice']>
```

❶   When instantiating a `Policy` you must pass in an indication of whether it is `open` or `closed` as well as a list of exceptions.

❷   Both `Tag` and `Namespace` objects have attributes corresponding to the related permissions. The instantiated object represents the `alice/rating` tag.

❸   Permissions for actions relating to a tag's values are referenced via `value_per missions`. Permissions relating to actions applying to the tag itself are accessed through the `permissions` attribute. In this case we're interested in the `read` action related to a tag's values.

❹   Assigning the new permission to the action causes FOM to update the permissions on the fly with Fluidinfo.

Tables 5-1, 5-2, and 5-3 outline the available actions for namespaces, tags, and a tag's values, along with the means of referencing them in FOM.

Table 5-1. Available permission actions for namespaces

Action name	Description
create	Controls whether a user can create new namespaces and tags within the referenced namespace
update	Allows a user to update the description of the namespace
delete	Indicates whether a user is allowed to delete the namespace
list	Controls whether a user can list the child namespaces and tags within the namespace
control	Indicates whether a user is allowed to control the permissions set on the namespace

Table 5-2. Available permission actions for tags

Action name	Description
update	Allows a user to update the description of the tag
delete	Indicates whether a user is allowed to delete the tag
control	Indicates whether a user is allowed to control the permissions set on the tag

Table 5-3. *Available permission actions for tag's values*

Action name	Description
create	Controls whether a user can create/update a value associated with an object via the tag
read	Allows a user to read a value associated with an object via the tag
delete	Indicates whether a user can delete a value from an object via the tag
control	Indicates whether a user is allowed to control the permissions set on the tag's values

Putting It All Together

This final section uses all the separate pieces of FOM that have been explored thus far to create a genuinely useful (and annotated) example of a Python script that could be adapted to import all sorts of different sorts of data into Fluidinfo.

For the purposes of defining a use case, imagine Alice has a list of books that she has read and that each book has an associated rating and comment. This might be an export of her data from one of the many book-related review sites on the Web. For the sake of argument, the data is stored in a CSV file that might be readable in any of the popular spreadsheet programs. Each row in the spreadsheet represents a book Alice has read. The only exception to this rule is that the very first row defines the following self-explanatory columns: title, authors, rating, and comment.

Furthermore, Alice needs to be able to rerun the script at any time (for the purpose of uploading updates) and wants to make sure that her ratings and comments are viewable only by herself and her friend Bert.

Finally, because she understands that there's already a convention for the about values used to reference objects representing books, she'll make use of the *abouttag* library to generate the about values that follow the usual *book title* convention.

The listing that follows is not the most idiomatic Python. The code has been written with readability and ease of comprehension in mind, especially for developers who are not familiar with Python:

```python
#!/usr/bin/env python
import csv
from getpass import getpass
from abouttag.books import book as aboutBook
from fom.session import Fluid
from fom.mapping import Object, Namespace, Tag, tag_value, Permission
from fom.errors import Fluid412Error


TAG_DEFINITIONS = {
    'title': 'The title of a book.',
    'author': 'The authors of a book.',
    'rating': 'What Alice thinks of a book on a scale of 1-10.',
    'description': "A description from Alice about a book she's read."
} ❶
```

```
class Book(Object): ❷
    """
    Represents a book in Fluidinfo.
    """

    title = tag_value('alice/books/title')
    author = tag_value('alice/books/author')
    rating = tag_value('alice/books/rating')
    description = tag_value('alice/books/description')
```

❶ Associates a tag name with a description. Used when creating the tags.

❷ The familiar Book class that inherits from FOM's Object class. Instances of these will represent each book to import.

```
def createSession(username):
    """
    Given a username, will ask for a password and create an appropriate session
    to use when connecting to Fluidinfo.
    """

    password = getpass("Password: ") ❶
    session = Fluid()
    session.login(username, password)
    session.bind() ❷
    return Namespace(username) ❸
```

❶ The getpass function is a useful way of safely prompting a user for his or her password.

❷ FOM binds to a session (an instance of the Fluid class). Notice how to pass the necessary user credentials through login.

❸ To be helpful, the function returns an object representing the user's top-level namespace.

```
def createTags(parentNamespace, tagDefinitions, exceptionsList):
    """
    Creates the tags defined in the tagDefinitions dictionary (where the key is
    the new tag's name and associated value is its description) within the
    namespace referenced by parentNamespace. The exceptionsList argument is a
    list of usernames indicating who should have read permission on the newly
    created tags.
    """

    p = Permission(policy='closed', exceptions=exceptionsList) ❶
    for tag, description in tagDefinitions.iteritems():
        try:
            newTag = parentNamespace.create_tag(tag, description)
            newTag.value_permissions['read'] = p ❷
            print "Tag '%s' created" % tag
        except Fluid412Error: ❸
            print "Tag '%s' already exists!" % tag
```

```
def createNamespace(parentNamespace, name, description):
    """
    Creates a new namespace with the given name and description in the parent
    namespace referenced by parentNamespace.
    """

    print "Creating namespace %s" % name
    try:
        return parentNamespace.create_namespace(name, description) ❹
    except Fluid412Error:
        print "Namespace '%s' already exists!" % name
        return Namespace('/'.join([parentNamespace.path, name])) ❺
```

❶   The instance of the Permission class that describes the new permission to be set on the tag.

❷   Assigning the new permission to the read action associated with the tag's values.

❸   Catching this exception means the script just continues if the tag already exists.

❹   Return the newly created namespace.

❺   Alternatively, if the namespace already exists, just return an appropriate instance of the Namespace class.

```
def getData(filename):
    """
    Opens a csv file, extracts the column names and builds a list of dictionary
    objects where each dictionary contains a key/value pair for each value in a
    particular row in the original CSV file.
    """

    csvReader = csv.reader(open(filename, 'rb'))
    columns = csvReader.next() ❶
    result = list()
    for row in csvReader:
        item = dict(zip(columns, [val for val in row])) ❷
        result.append(item)
    return result


def importData(data):
    """
    Iterates over a list of data dictionaries (one for each book), creates an
    appropriate object and annotates it with the correct tag values.
    """

    for item in data:
        aboutValue = aboutBook(unicode(item['title']), unicode(item['author'])) ❸
        book = Book(about=aboutValue)
        book.title = item['title']
        book.author = item['author']
        book.rating = item['rating']
        book.description = item['description']
```

```
        book.save() ❹
        print 'Imported %s' % aboutValue
```

❶   The column names just happen to be the same as the tag names.

❷   The zip method makes a dictionary-like object from two lists (the column names and the values for each row).

❸   Make use of the abouttag library to generate an appropriate fluiddb/about value for the object. The unicode function is used to ensure the characters are properly encoded.

❹   This call pushes the data to Fluidinfo.

```
def checkBooks(query):
    """
    Prints the number of Book objects matching the given query that have been
    imported so far (along with their titles).
    """

    results = Book.filter(query) ❶
    print '%d books imported into Fluidinfo so far:' % len(results)
    titles = [book.title for book in results]
    print '\n'.join(titles)


if __name__ == "__main__": ❷
    aliceNS = createSession('alice')
    bookNS = createNamespace(aliceNS, 'books', 'Contains tags about books.')
    exceptionsList = ['alice', 'bert']
    createTags(bookNS, TAG_DEFINITIONS, exceptionsList)
    data = getData('books.csv')
    importData(data)
    checkBooks('has alice/books/title')
    print 'Finished!'
```

❶   A simple query to allow us to check the number of books imported so far.

❷   If you're not familiar with Python, this is the equivalent of C's main function.

When run, the script will create output like the following:

```
$ ./import.py
Password: ***************
Creating namespace books
Tag 'rating' created
Tag 'author' created
Tag 'description' created
Tag 'title' created
Imported book book:the republic (plato)
Imported book book:flatland (edwin a abbot)
Imported book book:the dots and boxes game (berkelkamp)
Imported book book:how to lie with statistics (darrell huff)
Imported book book:blondie24 (david b fogel)
5 books imported into Fluidinfo so far:
The Dots and Boxes Game
```

```
The Republic
Blondie24
How to Lie with Statistics
Flatland
Finished!
```

FOM provides a convenient and familiar object-oriented view of Fluidinfo. However, there's more than one way to make a library developer-friendly, and *fluidinfo.js* (which we'll examine in the next chapter) does things very differently.

CHAPTER 6

Programming Fluidinfo with JavaScript

The *fluidinfo.js (https://github.com/fluidinfo/fluidinfo.js)* script is a small, self-contained library for using Fluidinfo in client-side JavaScript-based web applications.[1] Since Fluidinfo supports the emerging CORS (cross-origin resource sharing) standard (*http://www.w3.org/TR/cors/*), *fluidinfo.js* opens up the potential for sharing, using, and annotating open, linked data with Fluidinfo within your own web applications.

This chapter will be in two parts: a comprehensive description of *fluidinfo.js* followed by a detailed exploration of the steps taken to write a web-based book-reading application built using just *fluidinfo.js* and client-side JavaScript.

The *fluidinfo.js* library differs from the others examined so far in that it is asynchronous. It also provides developer-friendly capabilities through a set of functions to fulfill common tasks rather than an abstraction layer (like object orientation). These features are summarized in the following code snippet:

```
var options = {username: "alice", password: "secret"};
var session = fluidinfo(options);
var onSuccess = function(result) {
  // A callback to do something with the result
  console.log("OK");
  console.log(result);
};
var onError = function(result) {
  // A callback to handle when things go wrong
  console.log("ERROR");
  console.log(result);
};
session.query({
  select: ["fluiddb/about", "alice/rating", "alice/comment"],
```

---

1. The *fluidinfo.js* library is *framework agnostic*: it does not rely on any third party like jQuery or Moo to function. However, it can be used alongside such frameworks without any problems. It also works well in smartphone-based browsers.

```
        where: 'oreilly.com/title matches "Javascript"',
        onSuccess: onSuccess,
        onError: onError
    });
```

Notice how an `options` object containing credentials is passed into the `fluidinfo` function. If no credentials are supplied, all calls will be made as the anonymous user, which limits activity to objects with open permissions.

The return value of a call to the `fluidinfo` function is a session object. It provides various methods for using the raw API and for completing common tasks. In the preceding example, the `query` function is called to get values from objects that match the specified query. It's important to note that two callback functions are defined: `onSuccess`, which handles the result if the `query` call was a success, and `onError`, which is called in the event of an error of some kind. Finally, the `query` function (like all functions in the *fluidinfo.js* library) takes a single object argument specifying the various parameters that the function needs in order to succeed.

API Functions

The low-level API functions are the foundation of the library and are what the higher-level utility functions (described later) use to communicate with Fluidinfo. They can be referenced via the `api` attribute of the session object returned by the `fluidinfo` function and are named after the HTTP methods that they utilize.[2]

The API functions are uniform in the minimum options they require:

path
> The path to the endpoint being called; for example, `about/myobject/namespace/tag` (note how there's no leading slash). If part of the path needs to be safely URL-encoded, pass in a JavaScript array of the path's constituent parts, such as
>
> ```
> ["about", "my object", "namespace", "tag"]
> ```

onSuccess
> A function that takes a single argument (traditionally called `result`) whose task is to handle a successful response from Fluidinfo to the call being made

onError
> A function that takes a single argument (traditionally called `result`) whose task is to handle any errors raised by the call to Fluidinfo

---

2. Except for the `del` function, which uses the HTTP DELETE method since "delete" is a reserved word in JavaScript.

The object passed by the library to both the onSuccess and onError functions contains the following attributes:

status
> The HTTP status code for the result from Fluidinfo (for example, 200 or 404)

statusText
> A description of the status of the result from Fluidinfo (for example, "OK", "Not found")

headers
> An object representing the headers and associated values returned from Fluidinfo; for example,

```
{"Content-Type": "application/json"}
```

rawData
> If appropriate, a JavaScript string representation of the raw data payload returned from Fluidinfo (for example, the following JSON string: '{"id": "9c8e4b12-4b7d-40d2-865b-d5b1945350b1", "URL": "http://fluiddb.fluidinfo.com/objects/9c8e4b12-4b7d-40d2-865b-d5b1945350b1"}').

data
> If appropriate, a deserialized representation of the data payload returned by Fluidinfo (for example, a JavaScript object representation of the JSON string quoted above)

request
> A reference to the low-level XMLHttpRequest object used to coordinate the request (useful for the purposes of debugging)

The following examples show the general usage for each function according to the related HTTP action, along with comments on special features when appropriate.

DELETE

Making an HTTP DELETE call is simple. Just supply the path and callbacks to the del function:

```
var options = {
  path: "about/myobject/namespace/tag",
  onSuccess: function(result) {
    // handle success
  },
  onError: function(result) {
    // handle errors
  }
};
session.api.del(options);
```

Fluidinfo never returns any data from a del call.

GET

HTTP GET-based requests can require further arguments to be passed, which may need to be encoded in the URL:

```
var options = {
  path: "namespaces/alice",
  args: {
    returnDescription: true,
    returnTags: true
  },
  onSuccess: function(result) {
    // handle success
  },
  onError: function(result) {
    // handle errors
  }
};
session.api.get(options);
```

The example above results in the following URL:

http://fluiddb.fluidinfo.com/namespaces/alice?returnDescription=true&return
Tags=true

HEAD

The interesting thing about an HTTP HEAD call is that it only returns the headers of what would otherwise have been a GET call:

```
var options = {
  path: "about/avatar/alice/films/rating",
  onSuccess: function(result) {
    // handle success
  },
  onError: function(result) {
    // handle errors
  }
};
session.api.head(options);
```

Obviously, the useful information is found in the `result.headers` attribute.

POST

In order to pass data into Fluidinfo with an HTTP POST request you must specify a data attribute on the options object that you pass in to the function:

```
var options = {
  path: "namespaces/alice",
  data: {name: "films", description: "Contains tags about films."},
  onSuccess: function(result) {
    // handle success
  },
```

```
    onError: function(result) {
      // handle errors
    }
  };
  session.api.post(options);
```

Note how the data is passed in as a JavaScript object that *fluidinfo.js* automatically serializes for you.

PUT

As with the HTTP POST request, you must specify a `data` attribute on the options object:

```
var options = {
  path: "about/avatar/alice/films/comment",
  data: "<p>The Smurfs did the blue humanoid thing better.</p>",
  contentType: "text/html",
  onSuccess: function(result) {
    // handle success
  },
  onError: function(result) {
    // handle errors
  }
};
session.api.put(options);
```

Note how the MIME type of the value can be passed in via the (optional) `content Type` argument. If none is supplied, *fluidinfo.js* makes a sensible guess for you.

Utility Functions

The utility functions make it easy to perform the most common types of interaction with Fluidinfo. They follow exactly the same pattern as the `api`-based calls except for one important difference: the content of `result.data` will often be postprocessed by the function before being passed to your event handlers. This is usually to simplify and clean the data in some useful way.

Each function is an attribute of the session object returned from a call to the `fluid info` function described at the start of this chapter.

createObject

This function allows a logged-in user to create/reuse an object in Fluidinfo:

```
var options = {
  about: "my new object",
  onSuccess: function(result) {
    // handle success
  },
  onError: function(result) {
```

```
    // handle errors
  }
};
session.createObject(options);
```

The about value indicates what the new object represents. If an object with the same *about* value already exists, details of the existing object will be returned. It's possible to create so-called anonymous objects that don't have an associated *about* value by leaving the about attribute out of the options.

del

The del function removes a collection of tags (and associated values) from objects that match the query in the where argument:

```
var options = {
  tags: ["alice/rating", "alice/comment"],
  where: 'fluiddb/about="my object"',
  onSuccess: function(result) {
    // handle success
  },
  onError: function(result) {
    // handle errors
  }
};
session.del(options);
```

The example above removes the values associated with the alice/rating and alice/comment tags from the object whose *about* value is my object. Tags will be removed from *all* matching objects, but in this case, because all *about* values are unique, only one object will be changed.

getObject

This function returns a JavaScript object that represents an object in Fluidinfo with attributes for the specified tags/values. The Fluidinfo object can be referenced in two ways:

1. Using an *about* value:

```
var options = {
  about: "my object",
  select: ["alice/rating", "alice/comment"],
  onSuccess: function(result) {
    // handle success
  },
  onError: function(result) {
    // handle errors
  }
};
session.getObject(options);
```

2. Using an object's unique ID:

```
var options = {
  id: "9c8e4b12-4b7d-40d2-865b-d5b1945350b1",
  select: ["alice/rating", "alice/comment"],
  onSuccess: function(result) {
    // handle success
  },
  onError: function(result) {
    // handle errors
  }
};
session.getObject(options);
```

A successful response will have a single JavaScript object stored in the `result.data` attribute. This object will have attributes with the same name as the tags specified in the `select` clause passed in via the `options` object. It will also have the object's unique ID stored in the `id` attribute:

```
var obj = result.data;
var id = obj.id;
var aliceRating = obj["alice/rating"];
```

If a value is "primitive" (a number, Boolean, string, etc.), referencing the tag on the object (as shown here) will return the raw result. However, if the value is "opaque" (a binary value such as an image, audio, or PDF, or something with a MIME type of, for example, `text/html`), the result of referencing the tag on the object will be another object with three attributes:

value-type
: The MIME type associated with the value (for example, `image/png`)

size
: The size of the value

url
: A URL you can use to directly reference the value (this is useful if the value references an image and you need to work out how to set the `src` attribute of an `image` element to display it on a web page)

query

A successful call to the `query` function returns a JavaScript array of objects that match a specified query and whose attributes contain the specified tags:

```
var options = {
  select: ["alice/rating", "alice/comment"],
  where: "alice/rating > 6",
  onSuccess: function(result) {
    // handle success
  },
  onError: function(result) {
    // handle errors
```

```
    }
  };
  session.query(options);
```

Each object looks and behaves exactly like the single object described in "getObject" on page 72.

tag

The `tag` function allows users to attach values to specific objects. As with the `getObject` function ("getObject" on page 72), the object can be referenced in two ways: using its *about* value or its unique ID.

The values to be tagged are specified by an object identified by the **values** attribute of the options object:

```
var options = {
  values: {
    "alice/rating": 7,
    "alice/comment": "It's fantastic!"
  },
  about: "my object",
  onSuccess: function(result) {
    // handle success
  },
  onError: function(result) {
    // handle errors
  }
};
session.tag(options);
```

This function can be used to both add *and* change the values tagged to a *specific* object. To generalize this operation to several objects, use the **update** function described below.

update

This function updates the specified tags on *all* objects that match a query:

```
var options = {
  values: {
    "alice/rating": 10,
    "alice/comment": "It's fantastic"
  },
  where: 'alice/book/author matches "Lewis Carroll"',
  onSuccess: function(result) { // handle success },
  onError: function(result) { // handle errors }
};
session.update(options);
```

The example above sets the tag/values specified in the **values** object to all the objects that match the query specified in the **where** clause.

An Example Application: The Social Bookreader

This final section walks you through the steps needed to create a web-based application on Fluidinfo using *fluidinfo.js*. The application is a simple social "book" reader. The full source code is available on Github (*https://github.com/ntoll/bookreader*) and the application is hosted at http://bookreader.fluidinfo.com/ (*http://bookreader.fluidinfo .com/*).

The "book" to be displayed by the application is Becky Hogge's (*http://barefootintocy berspace.com/book/*) Creative Commons–licensed *Barefoot into Cyberspace*.[3] The code serves as both an example and a template for application developers, with three broad aims:

1. To display the content stored in Fluidinfo in a "book"-like fashion
2. To allow users to annotate the content of the "book"
3. To show what other users have annotated (tagged) onto the "book"

Why enclose the word *book* in quotation marks? Simply because the word represents a rather slippery concept in the digital context of Fluidinfo.

Modeling Data: What Is a Book?

The glib answer is that you're looking at one.

In reality, the answer requires more thought. For example, in this context, *book* does not mean a physical object consisting of pages of paper bound in codex form.

Perhaps the term means some sort of *work* that has at least one author whose thoughts are expressed as words organized into some sort of meaningful structure. Unfortunately, this isn't a good enough definition: it's both too broad and too specific. One could argue that poems and shopping lists fall under this definition (both are words organized into some sort of meaningful structure), whereas *comics* don't (because they depend heavily on pictures as well as words).

This philosophical diversion illustrates that it is important to explore and come to some sort of understanding of a problem domain. Such an understanding will probably be incomplete or even wrong, and in any case, the problem domain under scrutiny may also change over time. Therefore, *any solution* created to work with and model a problem is likely to be incomplete or simply not fit for all purposes.

This highlights one of Fluidinfo's great strengths: if you don't like what we do with the concept of *book* in this example application, you are entirely free to grab our data, remodel it to your satisfaction, and make it available to everyone else. If users prefer your mode of working with a *book*, they will copy your conventions rather than ours.

---

3. Used with permission from Becky.

As a result, evolutionary pressure is brought into the realm of data modeling (the fittest solutions are those that become most widely used).

With this in mind, here's how we model *Barefoot into Cyberspace* in Fluidinfo.

Granularity

By *granularity* we mean the level of detail that an individual object should represent. Should there be an object for every word? There certainly could be. In a sense this is already true. Several dictionaries have been imported into Fluidinfo so there are already objects for many words in the English language. Would it be sensible to model our problem at this level of detail?

Clearly not.

Return to our advice in Chapter 3: if you can name things with proper nouns, you probably want to map such things to objects in Fluidinfo. By this principle, obvious candidates to be represented by objects are the work itself (whose *about* tag would follow the naming convention for books), the constituent chapters (whose about tags would either reflect the chapter's title or numeric order within a work—for example, `barefootintocyberspace:chapter:1`), and the author (whose *about* tag value would follow the naming convention for authors).

Yet there are other things that constitute a book: paragraphs, headings, references, figures, individual sentences, and footnotes, for example. It is conceivable that users will want to tag individual paragraphs (as a summary of a concept, for instance) or sections of a work (a favorite chapter, perhaps).

Representing all the different types of things that make a book seems sensible. However, making a distinction between such types would introduce the potential for inconsistency and an inevitably complicated schema. The task of organizing, relating, and structuring such objects would be a minefield. In the next section we'll develop a simple, extendable structure for handling the complexity of the book concept.

Structure

Books are organized in a multitude of different ways, ranging from a simple linear structure (one paragraph followed by another) to works with chapters, footnotes, headings, figures, pictures, and so on. Put simply, we need to solve the problem of modeling the way authors organize things. For example, this is the third sentence in the first paragraph of the second subsection of the first subsection of the third top-level section in the sixth chapter of the book *Getting Started with Fluidinfo*. Many of the *blocks* described in the previous sentence also have names assigned to them (for example, the title of this subsection is "Structure"), and if we were to draw these relationships, we would end up with a tree-like structure with the *book as a whole* as the root. The complexity of the structure of the book would be visible in the number of branches in the resulting tree.

Given the desired granularity just described (encompassing the high-level book view down to the low-level paragraph view), how can a book be represented in such a way that *no matter what its structure is*, the schema used is both simple and uniform?

The solution is to link child objects in the tree to their parents with a `parent` tag whose value is the *about* value of the parent object. The position of the objects within their parent can be stored using a `position` tag and the content of the node in another appropriately named tag. In this way, objects that represent chapters would have a `parent` tag whose value was `book:barefoot into cyberspace (becky hogge)` (the *about* value of the object representing the complete work). Likewise, individual blocks would have parent tags containing the *about* value of the parent chapter.

This scheme is simple, yet powerful enough for our purposes. For example, to find all the blocks in the prologue chapter, one need only ask for objects that match `has beckyhogge/parent = "prologue"`. To find out the content and order of the matching blocks, one need only request the values of the `beckyhogge/html` and `beckyhogge/position` tags.

The queries just shown introduce another important aspect of the structure of the work: the tags are under the control of Becky via her `beckyhogge` account. She is expressing her opinion as author of what the structure and content of the book should be. However, since the objects are openly writable, there's nothing to stop me from adding my own (re)ordering, alternative wording (perhaps a translation), or even supplemental material (images and references) to the work as values under my own namespace. Of course, users would probably be interested only in Becky's version of the work (she is, after all, the author) and could safely ignore my contributions. The important point is that users opt in to whose version of the work they decide to use. The bookreader application currently only allows readers to view Becky's version.

Determining the structure of the work also involves choosing a naming convention for *about* values. The *about* values must be unique, understandable to both humans and machines, and predictable, and they will ideally express the block's place within the structure of the work. Given the emerging convention of using colon-separated items (for example, `book:animal farm (george orwell)`) as values for *about* tags, the obvious thing to do is construct a URI-like path that looks similar.

The naming convention for *about* values in our book structure is simply: `barefootintocyberspace:CHAPTER:POSITION` where `CHAPTER` and `POSITION` are replaced by a chapter's short name and block's position respectively (and as required to the appropriate depth). For example, the object whose about value is `barefootintocyberspace:prologue:2` represents the second block of text in the prologue.

Barefoot into Cyberspace is available in several different formats, the most immediately useful being the HTML at the book's website (*http://barefootintocyberspace.com/book/hypertext/*). This was downloaded, cleaned (removing everything but the elements containing the text of the work), and turned into a JSON representation of the structure of the work (a list of JSON objects for each block of text with attributes such as `position`, containing an integer indicating the block's place, and `html`, containing a string representation of the block's HTML). Furthermore, the work also includes various references that were also added to the appropriate objects. This structured version of the work was consumed by a simple script to import the work into Fluidinfo (the script was very similar to the one at the end of Chapter 5).

With this in mind, the following tags and associated values were used to annotate the different objects in Fluidinfo that represent the building blocks that constitute *Barefoot into Cyberspace*:

`beckyhogge/html`
> The HTML content of the block represented by the tagged object. To ensure that the content of the work is searchable, it was stored as a primitive `string` value rather than an (unsearchable) opaque value with the associated `text/html` MIME type.

`beckyhogge/licence`
> A URL pointing to the license that covers the block.

`beckyhogge/work`
> A reference to the object about the work, denoting the entire *Barefoot into Cyberspace*. This makes it easy to get the content of the whole book in a single simple query: `beckyhogge/work = "book:barefoot into cyberspace (becky hogge)"`.

`beckyhogge/parent`
> The all-important reference to the block's parent object.

`beckyhogge/position`
> An integer value indicating the position of the block within its parent block.

`beckyhogge/references`
> An array of any references contained within the block to other items.

Finally, given that the application allows any registered user to annotate comments onto the blocks of text, we should ask ourselves how to handle this. Happily, a `comment` convention already exists. Unfortunately it is only possible to attach one instance of a tag per object, and we want users of the application to annotate as many times as they like on a single block.

One possible solution is to use the `list` primitive type. This allows users to store an ordered list of strings. However, we'd like users to be able to do text matching on their comments and, unfortunately, this isn't possible on individual items in a list (yet).

The only way to do text matching is to store comments as primitive `string` values. In our solution we use the user's `comment` tag for this purpose. But how do we solve the problem of allowing users to add one or more comments to an object? After all, there can only be one `comment` tag from each user per object and only primitive string values can be matched. We solve this problem by *pretending* the single `comment` string is a list by delineating comments with the ¶ (pilcrow) character. The results look like this:

```
Fri, 13 Jan 2012 21:50:57 GMT
Comment 1
¶
```

Fri, 13 Jan 2012 21:51:01 GMT
Comment 2

Notice how each comment starts with its creation time, expressed as a human-readable and machine-readable version of universal time. The comment starts on the next line and continues until the pilcrow is reached.

This method of storing comments has several benefits:

- We're able to reuse the existing `comment` tag convention.
- Comments are searchable with the `matches` keyword in Fluidinfo's query language.
- Comments are both human and machine readable, yet contain all the required information (date and comment).
- It's simple.

Viewing Data: The User Interface

The user interface is very simple (see Figure 6-1).

Figure 6-1. The basic elements of the reader's user interface.

The navigation bar across the top of the screen contains links to the chapters (under the *Contents* drop-down menu) and other generic features of a website. The navigation bar is visible at all times as the user scrolls down the page to read the content.

The content takes up the rest of the screen. Next to each block of text is a small tag icon with a number next to it. The number indicates how many participants have annotated the associated block (*not* the total number of comments). Clicking the tag displays the comments annotated to the block of text (see Figure 6-2).

If the user is logged in, a form is also shown that allows him or her to annotate a comment to the block of text. Furthermore, the comments annotated by the logged-in

Figure 6-2. Displaying the annotations on a block of text.

user have an additional *delete* link next to the date and time of the comment. Clicking on it deletes the comment.

At the bottom of the screen are two buttons, Previous and Next, that allow users to move forward and backward between chapters.

The bookreader application consists entirely of HTML and client-side JavaScript. The only backend is Fluidinfo itself and the web server delivering static content. As a result, all the different user interface elements described previously raise *events* that are handled by the client and ultimately end up with calls to *fluidinfo.js*.

Application Logic: Putting It Together

The application logic that handles the user interface events is all found in the *book-reader.js* file. It contains many event handlers that deal with all the different ways a user might interact with the application. However, we're going to explore only events that result in calls to Fluidinfo via the *fluidinfo.js* library described at the start of this chapter.

Reading books

The most important function of the application is to allow users to read the book that's stored in Fluidinfo. When a link to a chapter is clicked, the following code is fired:

```
var options = {
    select: ["beckyhogge/html", "beckyhogge/position", "beckyhogge/references",
        "fluiddb/about"],
    where: 'beckyhogge/parent ="'+chapterName+'"',
    onSuccess: onSuccess,
    onError: onError
};
session.query(options);
```

The `session` object is the result of a call to the `fluidinfo` function, as described at the start of this chapter.

The `options` object simply defines the tag values to select in Fluidinfo, the query to run to match the objects whose tags need to be read (the `chapterName` variable is simply the short name of the chapter, which is taken from the `href` attribute of the link that raised the event), and the two expected callbacks to handle either a successful outcome or an error.

The application has a general purpose `onError` callback that is used everywhere. It simply displays an "Oops" message along with details of the result returned from Fluidinfo.

The `onSuccess` callback (not shown) does three things with the result before it's added to the DOM:

1. It orders the objects using the integer value stored by the `beckyhogge/position` tag.
2. It renders the `beckyhogge/html` value with an appropriate template that also creates the tag icon link.
3. It adds event handlers to the newly rendered element. This includes callbacks to handle the tag icon and clicking on a reference link.

The `onSuccess` callback also makes a further set of asynchronous function calls, each of which makes a call to Fluidinfo to count the number of participants that have tagged each object. When these figures have been returned, a further event handler adds them to the user interface.

Finally, an event handler is added to each of the Previous and Next buttons at the bottom of the screen. These are raised if the buttons are clicked and cause exactly the same code described earlier to fire, but for the appropriate chapter.

Annotating books

The relatively simple process in the previous section displays a chapter in the user's browser. In addition to simply reading the chapter, the user can interact with the application in three different ways:

1. By retrieving comments attached to a specific block of text (fired by clicking on the tag icon)

2. By creating new comments to be annotated on a block of text (fired by submitting the *Annotate this!* form)

3. By deleting unwanted comments (fired when the *delete* link next to a comment's timestamp is clicked)

Retrieval of comments is a two-step process: get an array of all the tags attached to the object representing the block of text, and then get the values of tags that match the username/comment pattern. This chain of requests is shown here:

```
var onSuccess = function(result){
    var commentTags = ['fluiddb/about'];
    var i;
    for(i=0; i<result.data.tagPaths.length; i++) {
        var tag = result.data.tagPaths[i];
        // use the commentMatcher regex to check the tagPath.
        if(tag.match(commentMatcher)){
            // it must be a comment tag path.
            commentTags.push(tag);
        }
    }
    if(commentTags.length > 1) {
        // only make the request if there are matching tags.
        var tagValOptions = {
            about: aboutBlock,
            select: commentTags,
            onSuccess: showComments,
            onError: onAnnotateError
        }
        session.getObject(tagValOptions);
    } else {
        // there were no matching tags so fake an empty result.
        showComments({data:[]});
    }
}
session.api.get({
    path: "about/"+aboutBlock,
    onSuccess: onSuccess,
    onError: onAnnotateError
});
```

The function that ultimately displays the comments (or a message to indicate that there are no comments) is showComments, which expects an object with a data attribute containing an array of comments. This function is called in two places: as the onSuccess function passed into the getObject call to grab the comments attached to the block of text and in the else clause reached if there are no comments (notice how an empty array is passed in to the function).

In a sense, the code reads the wrong way round, because the first thing to be executed is the last thing to be defined (the call to session.api.get at the bottom). Notice how the second step to fetch the comment values is executed only if it is needed. Otherwise, the result to showComments is *faked* through an empty array, as described earlier.

When a new comment is added to an object, it fires a simple tagging operation:

```
var saveComments = function(options) {
    var stringValue = packComments(options.commentList);
    var tagPath = options.author+"/"+commentTag;
    var values = {};
    values[tagPath] = stringValue;
    var tagOptions = {
        values: values,
        about: options.about,
        onSuccess: function(result){
            myComments = options.commentList;
            options.onSuccess(result);
            countParticipantComments(options.about);
        },
        onError: options.onError
    }
    session.tag(tagOptions);
};
```

The options object contains an array of the logged-in user's comments for the current block of text (commentList), the name of the user (the author attribute), the *about* value for the block of text, and references to the onSuccess and onError functions to call after attempting to save the comments.

The onSuccess function supplied by the options object is itself wrapped in an anonymous function to update the myComments array (which is an in-scope variable used to track the user's comments) and fire the countParticipantComments function to update the counter next to the appropriate tag icon.

Finally, deletion can happen in two ways:

1. If the user is deleting a comment but still has others attached to the block of text, the revised array of comments is updated in Fluidinfo using the saveComments function shown earlier.

2. Alternatively, if the user has no more comments attached to the object, the instance of the user's comment tag is removed from the object with the following simple block of code:

```
session.api.del({
    path: ["about", annotation.about, annotation.author, commentTag],
    onSuccess: function(result){
        myComments = [];
        cleanUpDelete();
        countParticipantComments(annotation.about);
    },
    onError: function(result){
        deleteAnchor.removeAttr("disabled");
        onAnnotateError(result);
```

```
        }
    });
```

Notice how the path to the tag to be deleted is passed in as an array that *fluidinfo.js* parses for you. Both the onSuccess and onError functions set the user interface to a state appropriate for the result.

Next Steps

The bookreader application is relatively simple and provides an opportunity for developers to play and create enhancements. The following ideas are left as exercises for the reader:

1. Make the application work with *any* book that is stored in Fluidinfo using the schema described in this chapter.

2. Allow readers to contribute and consume more than just simple comments. Ratings, links, images, and other assets should be viewable in a fashion similar to the way Twitter lets users view referenced material from around the Web (such as embedded YouTube videos or photographs from Flickr).

3. Allow readers to choose whose version of a work is to be displayed in the main reading view. For example, a reader might want to read Becky's text with inline images taken from the ntoll/picture tags attached to objects.

4. Enable users to contribute alternative versions of the text. This would be especially helpful for translation purposes.

The source code is open source and copiously commented. Explore, ask questions, play, and use your imagination!

CHAPTER 7

Fluidinfo's RESTful API

This chapter is meant as a reference for developers who want or need to work with Fluidinfo at the very lowest level: that of the HTTP API. It will be of special interest to developers who would like to write or enhance a client library for Fluidinfo.

The definitive documentation for the API is always at the Fluidinfo website (*http://api .fluidinfo.com/*). This chapter is a practical complement to it.

Fluidinfo's API is RESTful and uses HTTP as the underlying protocol for transfer of data between client and server. Resources within Fluidinfo are referenced by unique URIs, data is passed with an associated MIME type (usually JSON), and operations are done via HTTP methods such as POST, GET, PUT, and DELETE.

It is assumed that the reader has a basic understanding of HTTP, MIME types, and JSON, because the following sections are illustrated with examples of raw HTTP calls and responses given correctly constructed requests.

Making HTTP Requests to Fluidinfo

Fluidinfo expects requests and responses to have the following common requirements fulfilled.

User Validation

Fluidinfo currently uses basic HTTP authentication, although this is likely to change in the not-too-distant future.

This means that in order to send a request from a specific user, the client needs to send an Authorization header and associated token. It is also recommended that *all requests be made using SSL*, because that makes it possible to decode a user's credentials from the supplied token.

The authorization token is created by sending the string `Basic` followed by a space and then the appropriate username and password, separated by a single colon (:) character encoded as base64 data.

Of course, if the request is made as an anonymous user, the `Authorization` header should not be sent as part of the request.

Request Headers

In addition to the `Authorization` header, Fluidinfo expects certain other headers depending on the type of request being made.

There should always be an `Accept` header set to something convenient like */* (meaning the client will handle data of all media types returned from Fluidinfo). Many of the calls to Fluidinfo respond only with JSON data so, strictly speaking, such calls could have an `Accept` value of `application/json`.

Any requests that send data to Fluidinfo with the HTTP `POST` or `PUT` methods must supply two further headers: `Content-Type` and `Content-Length`.

The `Content-Type` header should indicate the type of data being sent to Fluidinfo. Again, most calls to Fluidinfo require the sending of JSON data, so the `Content-Type` value should be set to `application/json`. However, when dealing with raw tag values, the following considerations apply:

- When sending a JSON-encoded *primitive* type tag value (a value that is Boolean, null, string, numeric, or a list of strings), the `application/vnd.fluiddb.value+json` MIME type should be used.[1]

- When sending tag values that are of an *opaque* type (any other value), the `Content-Type` should be set to the most appropriate MIME value. For example, if the data is a PNG-encoded image, the associated MIME is `image/png`.

The `Content-Length` header indicates the size of the data being uploaded to Fluidinfo. It works exactly as described in the formal HTTP specification, RFC2616 (*http://www.ietf.org/rfc/rfc2616.txt*).

The important thing to note is that if these headers are not used as described here, or do not appear when required, Fluidinfo will return an HTTP `400` (`Bad Request`) response.

Response Headers

Fluidinfo responds to requests with the expected headers in order to conform to the HTTP specification. However, there are some unique features that you should be aware of.

---

1. The use of `fluiddb` is for historic reasons: it's the old name for Fluidinfo.

When dealing with tag values, the `Content-Type` header is an important indication of how to deal with the response. As you might guess, if the associated value is `applica tion/vnd.fluiddb.value+json`, the value in the body of the response will be a JSON-encoded *primitive* value. If it's anything else, the tag's value is an *opaque* value of the type specified by the `Content-Type` header.

In case of error, Fluidinfo will also return some custom headers to help the client discover, work out, and debug the cause of the problem. The most useful of these headers are `X-FluidDB-Path` (indicating the resource the error is connected to), `X-FluidDB-Mes sage` (a message about the error), and `X-FluidDB-Error-Class` (the name of the error). If the client is getting strange responses, these headers will cast some light on what's happening from Fluidinfo's point of view.

Encoding

Some requests that use the HTTP `GET` method need to pass information to Fluidinfo via arguments passed at the end of the URI. URIs can contain only two types of characters: *reserved* (those that have special meaning) or *unreserved* (those that do not have a special meaning but are a subset of the ASCII character set). Data to be passed into Fluidinfo via the URI *must be percent-encoded* to ensure that the URI doesn't contain any illegal characters.

For example, if you needed to send this query to Fluidinfo:

```
has ntoll/rating
```

the encoded version would look like this:

```
has%20ntoll%2Frating
```

Notice how the space and slash (/) characters have been replaced with `%20` and `%2F` respectively. Happily, practically every programming language has a module for escaping such characters. If you're interested in the details, take a look at the formal specification for URI syntax, RFC3986 (*http://tools.ietf.org/html/rfc3986*).

API Endpoints

Fluidinfo's API consists of a relatively few endpoints to which one makes an HTTP request. As mentioned earlier, Fluidinfo's API documentation (*http://api.fluidinfo .com/*) describes every possible call to each one of these endpoints and includes examples of the raw HTTP request and response.

The following sections give a brief overview of the purpose of each endpoint and, where required, highlight how they work when called by specific HTTP methods.

In general, the HTTP methods map to the following sorts of actions:

- POST requests create something new.
- GET requests retrieve data.
- PUT requests update values.
- DELETE requests delete things.
- HEAD requests provide information.

/about

The /about endpoint handles requests referring to a specific object *about* something (appended to the path). For example, sending a GET request to https://fluiddb.fluid info.com/about/big%20ben (note the correctly encoded *about* value) will return a JSON object containing information about the object (its ID and a list of attached tags that you have permission to read). Furthermore, if you append a tag's path to the URI and send a GET request,

```
GET /about/big%20ben/ntoll/comment HTTP/1.1
```

Fluidinfo will return the value for that tag on the referenced object:

```
HTTP/1.1 200 OK
Content-Length: 6
Date: Mon, 02 Aug 2011 13:20:31 GMT
Content-Type: application/vnd.fluiddb.value+json

"bong"
```

Sending a POST request to Fluidinfo will create a new object *about* the thing referenced in the URI. If there is already an object in Fluidinfo about the given value, details of the preexisting object will be returned.

Importantly, you can't remove objects from Fluidinfo once they're created because no one owns an object (because it is a shared resource). However, it is possible to use the DELETE method to remove tags from objects and the PUT method to annotate/update them on objects.

/namespaces

The /namespaces endpoint allows users to administer their namespaces. Happily, it works in exactly the way you would expect: POST requests create namespaces, GET requests retrieve information about namespaces, PUT requests update namespaces, and DELETE requests remove empty namespaces.

Every namespace can have a description to indicate the function of the namespace.

To refer to a namespace, simply append its path to the endpoint's URI. For example, a GET request to https://fluiddb.fluidinfo.com/namespaces/oreilly.com will return information about the oreilly.com namespace.

/objects

The /objects endpoint works in *exactly the same way* as the /about endpoint except for two important differences:

- Instead of referencing objects by their *about* value in the URI, you simply use the object's globally unique ID. For example, sending a GET request to https://fluiddb.fluidinfo.com/objects/9c8e4b12-4b7d-40d2-865b-d5b1945350b1 returns information about the referenced object.
- When creating a new object with a POST request, you can optionally indicate what the new object is about by sending the desired value in an appropriate JSON object as the payload of the request.

In general, it's better to use the /about endpoint, simply because it's easier to read and build meaningful URIs.

/permissions

The /permissions endpoint is used to control permissions relating to namespaces and tags. Only the GET and PUT methods can be used with this endpoint, because all you'll ever want to do is retrieve information about a permission or update a permission.

Permissions are inherited at the time of creation. When you create a new namespace or tag, the starting set of permissions is based on those associated with the newly created entity's parent namespace.

Permissions apply to actions associated with specific namespaces or tags. Possible actions depend on whether you're referring to a namespace or tag but are generally verbs such as create, update, read, and delete (the API documentation has the complete list).

Every action's permission is made up of two parts: the policy (which will be either open or closed) and the exceptions (a list of the names of Fluidinfo users who are exceptions to the policy).

The URIs use three indicators to tell Fluidinfo if you're referring to a namespace (indicated as namespaces), tag (tags), or values associated with a tag (tag-values). The path to the entity of interest is appended to the path after the appropriate indicator.

The action is passed as an argument appended to the URI.

For example, sending a GET request to https://fluiddb.fluidinfo.com/permissions/namespaces/oreilly.com?action=update will return the update permission for the oreilly.com namespace. The result will be some JSON that looks something like this:

```
{
  "policy": "closed",
  "exceptions": ["oreilly.com"]
}
```

This indicates that no one except O'Reilly can create new tags or namespaces within the `oreilly.com` namespace.

If O'Reilly wanted to give the Fluidinfo user `ntoll` the ability to create new tags or namespaces within `oreilly.com`, it would send a PUT request to the same URI with the following updated permission as the payload:

```
{
  "policy": "closed",
  "exceptions": ["oreilly.com", "ntoll"]
}
```

/tags

The `/tags` endpoint allows users to administer their tags. Exactly as with the `/namespaces` endpoint, it works the way you would expect: POST requests create tags, GET requests retrieve information about tags, PUT requests update tags, and DELETE requests remove tags.

Every tag can have a description, in case the context given by its name and parent namespace are not enough to indicate its function. The description is also a handy place to describe the *type* of data you'll be expecting to store using the tag. For example, a `rating` tag might have the following description, "Indicates how I feel about something, indicated by a number in the range of 1 (sucko barfo) to 10 (it's awesome!)."

To refer to a tag, simply append its path to the endpoint's URI. For example, a GET request to `https://fluiddb.fluidinfo.com/tags/ntoll/rating` will return information about the `ntoll/rating` tag.

Finally, upon creation of a tag, you are expected to set an `indexed` flag in the tag's specification described in a JSON object. Originally this was done to indicate whether values associated with the newly created tag were to be indexed for the purposes of text matching. However, Fluidinfo indexes *every* tag, so this flag is redundant and will be removed from the API in the not-too-distant future (it has been kept in so far only to maintain backward compatibility).

/users

Only one sort of request can be made to the `/users` endpoint. If you want to find out information about a specific user in Fluidinfo, simply send a GET request to the endpoint with the appropriate username appended. For example, sending a request to `https://fluiddb.fluidinfo.com/users/ntoll` will return information about the user called `ntoll` (their real name and the object ID for the object about `ntoll`).

/values

The /values endpoint allows you to work with several objects and tags at the same time. Only the GET, PUT, and DELETE methods, for retrieving, updating, and deleting data respectively, can be used. This is the Fluidinfo equivalent to SQL's SELECT, UPDATE, and DELETE statements.

As you'd expect, requests always involve a query to match the set of affected objects and a list of tags (and related values, in the case of a PUT request).

For example, updating a specific object with a set of new values would involve sending a PUT request to /values. All the information about the update is encapsulated in a JSON object that's sent as the request payload. It would look something like this:

```
{
  "queries": [
    [
      "fluiddb/about=\"big ben\"": {
        "ntoll/rating": {
          "value": 10
        },
        "ntoll/comment": {
          "value": "BONG!"
        },
        "ntoll/visited": {
          "value": true
        }
      }
    ]
  ]
}
```

This example updates the object about Big Ben with three values stored against ntoll's rating, comment, and visited tags.

It is important to note that only *primitive* values can be updated in this way, because JSON is not designed for the transmission of large amounts of binary data.

This also applies to the results returned from sending a GET request: Fluidinfo will return only primitive values. If a tag references an opaque value, Fluidinfo will return just the value's size and associated MIME type.

CHAPTER 8

Advanced Use of the Fluidinfo Shell

Chapter 2 provided an introduction to the Fluidinfo Shell (Fish) and an overview of its key commands. We now expand on this. We begin by looking at how to interrogate Fluidinfo's permissions system in more detail using the -G option to the ls command. We then discuss how Fish can be used to set more complex configurations of permissions using the -X option to the perms command. Finally, we introduce the -l and -g flags available with the ls command, which allow more compact and Unix-like "long" listings of tags and namespaces.

Permissions in Depth

As mentioned in Chapter 2, the view of permissions presented so far is a simplification. Fluidinfo in fact maintains several write permissions for tags and namespaces, and also two different control permissions for tags. Because the various write permissions are normally set identically, as are the control positions, this is not usually important. But in the minority of instances where this is not the case, the extra controls add considerable flexibility. If you don't care about the detail, you can safely skip the rest of this section.

In Chapter 2, we saw that ordinarily, the ls -L command produces output like this:

```
$ fish ls -Ld /alice /alice/rating

alice/:
     read: policy: open; exceptions = []
    write: policy: closed; exceptions = [alice]
  control: policy: closed; exceptions = [alice]


alice/rating:
     read: policy: open; exceptions = []
    write: policy: closed; exceptions = [alice]
  control: policy: closed; exceptions = [alice]
```

In order to view the permissions on a tag or namespace, the user has to have control permission over it. This means that you will get HTTP 401 errors (Unauthorized) if you try to look at permissions for most tags and namespaces that you don't own. The previous command was issued by the user Alice, who (not having surrendered control permissions) is able to view them.

Let's now look at the same command when a more intricate set of permissions has been used. Consider the case of the Fluidinfo user named fish, which is used by Shell-Fish, the online version of fish. The fish user allows access to Fluidinfo, including limited write permission, to users who do not have their own Fluidinfo account or who do not wish to use it with Shell-Fish. Let us look at the permissions on the fish user's top-level namespace and on its z tag:

```
$ fish ls -Ld /fish /fish/z

fish/:

NAMESPACE (/namespaces)
  Read
    list (read):        policy: open; exceptions = []
  Write
    create (create):    policy: closed; exceptions = [njr]
    update (metadata):  policy: closed; exceptions = [fish]
    delete (delete):    policy: closed; exceptions = [njr]
  Control
    control (control):  policy: closed; exceptions = [njr]

fish/z:

TAG (/tags)
  Write
    update (metadata):  policy: closed; exceptions = [fish]
    delete (delete):    policy: closed; exceptions = [njr]
  Control
    control (acontrol): policy: closed; exceptions = [njr]

TAG (/tag-values)
  Read
    read (read):        policy: open; exceptions = []
  Write
    create (tag):       policy: closed; exceptions = [fish]
    delete (untag):     policy: closed; exceptions = [fish]
  Control
    control (tcontrol): policy: closed; exceptions = [njr]
```

Although the command issued here has an identical structure to the previous one, the output is more complex, and it shows the set of permissions that Fluidinfo maintains for tags and namespaces in full detail. This longer listing is automatically generated by -L when the simpler view cannot accurately describe the permissions settings. That is true in this case because not all the write permissions are the same. This more detailed view can also be requested explicitly by using -G instead of -L; you might think of the G as standing for *glorious detail*, but it is really just a counterpart to -g (group), which will be introduced later.

Look first at the top-level namespace, fish. The output shows that there are five separate permissions for the namespace—one governing reading, three governing writing, and one governing control. For a namespace, the permissions have the following meanings:

read
> This governs the ability to list the items in the namespace (like the *x* execute permission on a Unix directory). There is only one read permission.

create
> This write permission governs whether new tags and sub-namespaces can be created within the namespace.

update
> This write permission governs whether the description of the namespace can be altered.

delete
> This write permission governs whether tags and sub-namespaces can be removed from the namespace.

control
> This permission determines who can alter the permissions on the namespace. There is only one control permission on namespaces.

In the output just shown, the read permission is open, which is its default, but the write and control permissions are nonstandard. All of the write permissions, as well as the control permission, would normally be closed except to the fish user, but in this case it is the njr user rather than fish who has the exclusive ability to create new (abstract) tags, to delete them, and to control the namespace. This is because njr is the creator of Fish. The fish user itself can only write the namespace's description.

The information looks somewhat repetitive, with permissions inside parentheses and outside parentheses:

    list (read)

The reason for this is that the names in parentheses are Fish's name for the permission in question, while the preceding names, outside the parentheses, are the names used in Fluidinfo's API for that permission. They are different partly because the parenthesized names are more fine-grained, and therefore more descriptive, but more importantly because in the case of tags, as we shall see shortly, some different permissions have the same name in the API, making them awkward to use in commands.

Look now at the permissions on the tag fish/z.

As you can see, there are seven separate permissions on tags, which Fluidinfo breaks into two groups, some of which are accessed in the HTTP API through the `/tags` endpoint[1] and others through `/tag-values`. Despite the apparent implication of this, all of the permissions govern whole (abstract) tags, not individual uses of a tag.

The read permission is straightforward and controls whether people can detect the presence of a tag on an object and read its value (if any).

The API's `create` permission on `/tag-values` controls the ability to tag an object using the tag; Fish calls this *tag permission*. Similarly, the permission the API calls `delete` on `/tag-values` controls the ability to remove a tag from an object; Fish calls this *untag permission*. In this case, the `fish` user has the exclusive ability to tag and untag objects.

The API's `update` permission on the endpoint `/tags` controls the ability to set the description for a tag; Fish calls this *metadata permission*. Finally, the permission that the API calls `delete` on `/tags` controls the ability to delete an abstract tag (which the API allows even if the tag is in use). Fish also calls this *delete* permission. In this case, the `fish` user can again change the description of the tag, but cannot delete the tag itself: only `njr` can do that. Thus, the net effect of the write permissions in combination is that `fish` can tag and untag objects using the tag `fish/z`, and change its description, but cannot delete the tag from the namespace.

The existence of two sets of control permissions simply reflects the division of permissions into two groups. The `acontrol` permission determines who can set the `update`/ `metadata` and `delete` permissions, whereas the `tcontrol` permission determines who can set the rest of the write permissions as well as the read permission.

Setting Individual Low-Level Permissions with perms -X

Individual write and control permissions can be set by adding the Fish name for the low-level permission (the one shown in parentheses in the detailed `ls -L` listing) after a `-X` option. For example, Alice could give herself, Bert, and Γλαύκων the ability to tag objects with her `private/fears` tag by entering this command:

```
$ fish perms write -X tag closed except alice+bert+γλαύκων private/fears
```

The `-X` option can be repeated, so she could simultaneously set the `tag` and `untag` permissions with this command:

```
$ fish perms write -X tag -X untag closed except alice+bert+γλαύκων private/fears
```

---

1. An *endpoint* is a top-level path under `http://fluiddb.fluidinfo.com`, used for reading from and writing to Fluidinfo. "The endpoint `/tags`" is a shorthand for `http://fluiddb.fluidinfo.com/tags`.

Generating Unix-style Long Listings with ls -l and ls -g

This section is primarily for people with good familiarity with Unix who are interested in a compact, Unix-like view of Fluidinfo permissions. Others may safely skip the section.

Unix users may well be hankering after a more compact view of the permissions, more akin to the sort of thing that can be generated by ls -l and ls -g on Unix. It turns out that, with some fairly natural mappings, Fluidinfo permissions can be reasonably described by a permissions string similar to that used on Unix. The mapping between the Unix permissions string and Fish's similar representation of Fluidinfo permissions is illustrated in Figure 8-1.

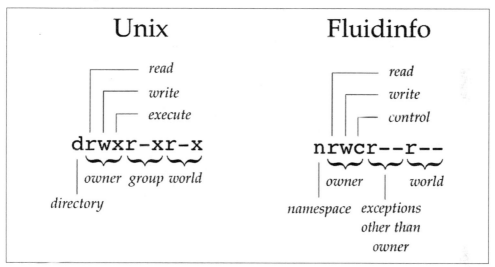

Figure 8-1. Mapping between a Unix permissions string and Fish's Fluidinfo permissions string

As in Unix, we use a ten-character string to represent the permissions. The first character is n for namespaces and t for tags. The remaining nine digits consist of three groups of three, the groups corresponding to the owner, to exception lists (excluding the owner), and to everyone else (world). Within each group, characters correspond to *read*, *write*, and *control* permissions, in that order. The possible values for the characters are the following:

r, w, *or* c
> Read, write, or control permission, respectively, is granted.

-
> The permission in that position is denied.

/
> The permission in that position is in a mixed state. This most commonly occurs with the write permission.

Default permissions for namespaces and tags are illustrated by Alice's top-level name-space, alice, and her rating tag:

```
$ fish ls -ld /alice rating
nrwcr--r--   alice/
trwcr--r--   alice/rating
```

The permissions on fish and fish/z form a more unusual case:

```
$ fish ls -ld /fish /fish/z
nr/-r/cr--   fish/
tr/-r/cr--   fish/z
```

Here we see from the owner permissions block, [r/-], that the owner (fish) has read permission, *some* write permissions, and no control permission. The next block, which shows nonowner exceptions, [r/c], shows that at least one user has read permission, *some* write permissions, and control permission. The final block, [r--], shows us that people other than the owner and the exceptions have read permission but no write or control permission.

We can get more detail on the exceptions group by using the -g option, instead of (or as well as) -l:

```
$ fish ls -gd /fish /fish/z
nr/-r/cr--   r:(world)  w:<variable>   fish/
tr/-r/cr--   r:(world)  w:<variable>   fish/z
```

In this case, however, there is no real extra information. The r:(world) simply confirms that the whole world has read permission, and w:<variable> means that different write permissions have different exception lists, so in this case we would actually have to use -L or -G to get the full picture.

A more typical example occurs with Alice's private/fears tag:

```
$ fish ls -g private/fears
trwcrw----   r:bert+γλαύκων  w:bert   alice/private/fears
```

Here we see that Alice has full access, Bert and Γλαύκων have both have read access, and Bert has write access, too.

If Alice were to grant write permission to Γλαύκων also, the view would simplify to

```
trwcrw----   bert+γλαύκων   alice/private/fears
```

since the read and write groups would then be the same.

For more detail on these listings, see the Fish documentation (*http://fluiddb.fluidinfo.com/about/fish/fish/index.html*) and the blog post "Setting and Changing Permissions with FDB" (*http://blog.abouttag.com/2011/06/setting-and-changing-permissions-with.html*) (which refers to fdb, the old name for Fish).

CHAPTER 9

Conventions for the About Tag

Fluidinfo guarantees that *about* tags (`fluiddb/about`) are unique and unchanging. These properties make the *about* tag an ideal identifier. Other tags attached to an object with a given *about* tag are clearly and unambiguously associated with whatever the *about* tag specifies. It is, however, important to understand that Fluidinfo ascribes no meaning to *about* tags or objects; there is no reference mapping between *about* tags and real-world objects, and there are no rules—only conventions—about which objects should be used to store data in Fluidinfo.

If your data is self-contained, in the sense that it is not combined with or dependent on any other user's tags, it does not matter very much which objects you use, though it would be perverse and somewhat antisocial to "pollute" objects having an *about* tag with data that does not pertain to it. As a general principle, if you are not choosing objects on the basis of their *about* tag, there is a strong case for using objects that have no *about* tag.

As we will see, for anyone who does wish to combine data with that from other Fluidinfo users, there are strong benefits from adopting conventions for tags, particularly *about* tags, and these benefits increase as more users adopt the same conventions.

A Book Example

Consider the case of a set of users who wish to share data on books. They have a number of choices. If there is a recognized leading or reference user who is going to take responsibility for trying to ensure that Fluidinfo contains objects for each possible book, and everyone agrees who that user is, it is possible simply to use that user's tags to identify the book of interest. For example, if ISBN decided to publish its entire book catalog to Fluidinfo, and to use `isbn.org/title` and `isbn.org/author` to identify books, it would be natural for other users to use the same objects. Even in this case, however, there are a number of difficulties that other users would face in choosing which object to use for a particular book if the *about* tag, with appropriate conventions, were not adopted by `isbn.org`. These would include:

- While ISBN covers a large number of books, its coverage is not complete.
- Unless ISBN updates Fluidinfo in a very regular and timely manner, other users may find themselves needing to wait for ISBN to create the relevant object before being able to add information to it.
- Even if the relevant object has been created by ISBN, it will not necessarily be easy to locate it, especially programmatically. We would need to know things such as
  —How capitalization is handled (`The Book Thief, THE BOOK THIEF, The book thief`...?)
  —How punctuation is handled (`J. D. Salinger; JD Salinger; J.D. Salinger; Salinger, J. D.`...?)
  —Whether articles are moved to the end of titles (`The Book Thief` or `Book Thief, The`)
  —How accents and punctuation are handled (`Louis-Ferdinand Céline, Louis Ferdinand Céline, Louis Ferdinand Céline, Louis Ferdinand Celine`, ...?)

One part of the problem is knowing exactly how to construct the values of the relevant tags (in this case, author and title) from the values that you actually possess, perhaps in a database or on the book itself. Resolving this requires conventions about how text is normalized. Ideally, this is solved by everyone using the same normalization algorithm to construct the identifying tag values. (The *abouttag.py* library, discussed later in this chapter, provides some help here.)

The second part of the problem arises if you want to use an object that does not already exist—in this case, if ISBN hasn't created it yet. This problem is neatly solved by the *about* tag: if you know that when ISBN *does* store its data about *Getting Started with Fluidinfo*, it will use the object with the *about* tag `book:Getting Started with Fluidinfo (nicholas j radcliffe; nicholas h tollervey)`, you can tag the object before ISBN does.

A third aspect of the problem is that there is nothing to guarantee that only one object will have the `isbn.org/author="Anne Michaels"` and `isbn.org/title="Fugitive Pieces"`; in fact, in this case, that is unlikely, because international standard book numbers identify individual *publications* of books, rather than operating at the level of the conceptual work. That is, there are many ISBN numbers for *Fugitive Pieces* by Anne Michaels (978-0747534969, 978-0747529392, and 978-0747599258, among others). This illustrates another aspect of storing information in Fluidinfo, namely that different objects might correspond to different levels of specificity, since it is entirely legitimate to want to store data either about the conceptual work *Fugitive Pieces*, or about a particular publication of that book (the 1997 Bloomsbury UK softcover edition, for example).[1]

---

1. The interested reader is referred to an excellent paper, "What is FRBR? A Conceptual Model for the Bibliographic Universe" by Barbara Tillett, available from the Library of Congress Cataloging Distribution Service.

Using the *about* tag to identify the object has several advantages. First, it is not necessary for anyone to have created an object before it is used: in effect, it is created the first time a user uses it.[2] Secondly, the uniqueness of the *about* tag means that two unconnected users will, if following the same convention, automatically end up using the same object. The resulting grouping of related information and its potential recombination in ways possibly unanticipated by the people who added it to Fluidinfo is an important and deliberate design feature of Fluidinfo.

Finally, the immutability of the *about* tag means that users can have confidence that the object that they tag will not mutate in identity: even if ISBN gets hacked, or taken over by someone with peculiar plans, because it is Fluidinfo itself that guarantees the uniqueness and immutability of the *about* tag, users are assured that their data will remain associated with the same *about* tag and, to the extent that stable conventions are adopted for *about* tags, to the same real-world object.

The Perfect About Tag

Simplistically, our goal is create a perfect correspondence between real-world entities and Fluidinfo objects, and for everyone to agree which Fluidinfo object corresponds to each thing in the real world. This goal is not fully realizable, but with careful forethought and planning we can devise conventions that allow us to approach this situation.

Ideally, our *about* tags should have the following properties:

- It should be easy to construct a well-defined, unique *about* tag for any entity, preferably without needing to refer to any external information.
- Different people and applications, at different times, should construct the same *about* tag.
- The *about* tags for different real-world entities should be different.
- The *about* tag should be meaningful to a human.

If we achieve these goals, we can avoid two problems that will otherwise reduce the power of Fluidinfo. The first is *fragmentation*, which arises if different people use different Fluidinfo objects to store information about the same real-world entity. This is a familiar problem in many areas; for example, when using Gracenote, the CD database looked up by iTunes and other services when a CD is read by a computer, it is common to find the same artist represented different ways on different CDs, and even for there to be several, slightly incompatible listings for a single CD.

---

2. There is an alternative way of thinking about objects in Fluidinfo that is philosophically pleasing. In this view, an object for every possible *about* tag already exists, but Fluidinfo instantiates them only lazily, when a user references them, usually by tagging. This lazy instantiation may be regarded as an implementation detail.

The obverse of that problem is *overloading*, which describes the situation in which information about different things is stored on the same object. This is also a serious problem. As a trivial example, if we simply store data on objects using the natural English name as the *about* tag, we might store information about both the planet Mercury and the element mercury on the same object. Needless to say, this could lead to serious confusion, especially if we store properties like mass.

Normalization and Standardization

Some of the more widely used conventions for *about* tags in Fluidinfo today follow a general pattern typified by the `book-u` convention illustrated above:

- They map terms to lowercase and remove most punctuation but preserve accents.
- They begin with a keyword that identifies the class of object followed by a colon (for example, `book:` for books and `album:` for albums).
- They include at least one identifier that helps to disambiguate different objects that would otherwise map to the same *about* tag.

Examples of such conventions include those for books, albums, tracks, and films, such as the following:

```
book:nineteen eighty four (george orwell)
album:the dark side of the moon (pink floyd)
track:summertime (billie holiday)
film:the postman always rings twice (1946)
```

While not absolutely guaranteeing uniqueness, these conventions make clashes extremely rare, while using only data that is readily available to almost anyone possessing or having access to the item in question.

All parts are needed: without the "book," we could be referring to the book or the film of *Nineteen Eighty-Four*. Without the year, we could be referring to either of two films called *The Postman Always Rings Twice*.

Ideally, for any convention, the algorithm should be documented and published, preferably in the form of a library and an accompanying web service, so that everyone can construct identical *about* tags through a process of normalizing inputs in a systematic way. The *abouttag.py* library, for this purpose, is available from Github (*http://github.com/njr0/abouttag*), or using the Python Package index, `pypi`, if you have `pip` installed:

```
$ pip install -U abouttag
```

It covers the previous conventions and many others, is open source, is included with the Fish utility used in Chapter 2, and is also the basis of a web service available at *http://abouttag.com*. It also includes functions for performing generic normalization, making it easy to add new conventions similar to those already there.

An alternative way of generating *about* tags, or conventions for them, is to rely on an external source. For example, every page from the English-language edition of

Wikipedia has been imported to Fluidinfo with *about* tags chosen based on simply taking the Wikipedia page title and mapping it to lowercase. In Wikipedia, there is a page for *Nineteen Eighty-Four*, with that exact title, so if you look in Fluidinfo at the object with *about* tag nineteen eighty-four, you see a pointer to the relevant web page:

```
$ fish tags -a 'nineteen eighty-four'
Object with about="nineteen eighty-four":
  /en.wikipedia.org/url = "http://en.wikipedia.org/wiki/Nineteen_Eighty-Four"
```

Specificity, Ambiguity, and Language

Even following these guidelines, many questions remain, and they can be settled in different ways. Perhaps the two most challenging issues are specificity and language.

As humans, we frequently use the same label for multiple things, relying mostly on context and common sense to disambiguate, clarifying only when confusion arises or the ambiguity is particularly acute. This works less well in the digital realm, because if the data is stored ambiguously, it can be hard or impossible to disambiguate it later. In the case of all the four items discussed above, the level explicitly chosen for the *about* tags is the *conceptual work*—the book George Orwell wrote, entitled *Animal Farm*, the album Pink Floyd made called *The Dark Side of the Moon*, the song Billie Holiday recorded called "Summertime," and the 1946 film *The Postman Always Rings Twice*. These objects do not refer to specific editions of the work—publications of the book, formats for the album, particular albums on which the song appeared, or media on which the film was released.

The level of the conceptual work was chosen for these initial conventions because it is the level most people typically have in mind when they want to annotate or pass comment on these kinds of cultural works. There are certainly cases in which we want to differentiate between editions or recordings, but when we say "*Nineteen Eighty-Four* is one of the most important books of the twentieth century," we are clearly talking about the work, and ordinarily, if someone wanted to rate a book, it would be the work rather than the edition that would be of interest. Fluidinfo is entirely agnostic on these points, and other conventions not only *can* be created for other levels of the hierarchy, but actually *have been,* albeit in a less systematic manner.

Languages

All textual data in Fluidinfo is stored as Unicode, meaning that all international characters can be used. The names of tags, namespaces, and users are also Unicode, and they may contain any alphabetic characters from any language or combination of languages, as well as digits and certain punctuation characters. So other than the fact that the API commands have English names, and the Fluidinfo superuser (fluiddb) uses English tag names, Fluidinfo itself is entirely language-neutral.

There is, however, a large, unresolved issue about languages in Fluidinfo. This core question is:

> Is it better to group information in multiple languages but concerning the same real-world entity on the same object or to have a set of related objects for the same real-world entity in different languages, probably with cross-references?

There are significant advantages and disadvantages of both approaches. While numeric data is obviously largely language-neutral, textual data is not. The advantage, in terms of completeness of having multilingual data in one place, is rather offset by the confusion most people have sifting through information in languages they don't know.

Perhaps a more significant issue is the choice of tag names and *about* tag values. The advantage of using highly readable (English) *about* tags like `book:animal farm (george orwell)` is obviously entirely reversed for a native Japanese speaker.

At the time of writing, most of the data being added to Fluidinfo is in English, and this issue is not really being actively tackled, but it seems likely that largely separate objects will be used in different languages, just as in Wikipedia there are separate editions.

Tags for Indicating Related Objects (Linking)

It is common to want to create links between objects in Fluidinfo, and this is easy to do. For objects that have *about* tags, the obvious way to achieve this is simply to tag one object with the *about* tag for the other, using the name of the tag to indicate the nature of the relationship. For example, the `musicbrainz.org` user uses this mechanism to link artists and albums.

If we look at the object for the album *Strange Fruit*, by Billie Holiday (Figure 9-1, top), we see that it has a tag called `related-artists` that links this album to its artist—in this case, `artist:billie holiday`, the object in the middle. Similarly, if we look at the object whose *about* tag is simply `Billie Holiday` (bottom) we see a tag `related-albums`, linking to the more specific object for the artist, and also one to the album called *Billie Holiday,* having the *about* tag `album:billie holiday (billie holiday)`.[3]

This use of tags with names that start `related-` is quite widespread within Fluidinfo. Where there is potential for multiple related objects, the noun following `related-` is usually chosen to be plural, as in these cases (`related-artists`, `related-albums`) and the tag's value is a *list* of *about* tags. Where there is only one related item—for example, most people have only one father—the singular form is more commonly used (`related-father`), usually with a simple string value rather than a list of strings.

The `related-` convention is particularly helpful to allow Fluidinfo objects with rather general *about* tags to act as disambiguation nodes with links to other more specific

---

3. In this case, the MusicBrainz user has made this link because the title of the album is *Billie Holiday*, though it would also, of course, be possible to link to all albums by Billie Holiday.

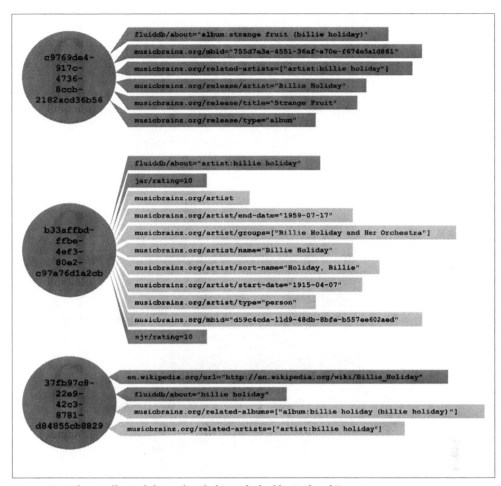

Figure 9-1. Three Billie Holiday–related objects linked by "related-" tags

items. So, for example, the object with the *about* tag nineteen eighty four has various related- tags attached to it, as we can see:

```
$ fish tags -a "nineteen eighty four"
Object with about="nineteen eighty four":
  /fluiddb/about = "nineteen eighty four"
  /musicbrainz.org/related-albums = {"album:nineteen eighty four (crucifix)"}
  /musicbrainz.org/related-tracks = {"50b5d67a-3b6d-4555-aae9-bc9aabcfe247",
"8f9bafc7-28fe-4967-a66e-7f2b76e395ad"}
  /njr/related-book = "book:nineteen eighty four (george orwell)"
  /njr/related-film = "film:nineteen eighty four (1984)"
```

One points to an object for the book, one to the film, one to albums, and one to tracks. (Notice that the last uses object IDs, since those objects have no *about* tags.) It is entirely possible that some people will choose to store data about the more specific examples of *Animal Farm* on this object (particularly the book, that being probably the most common association for the term), and the existence of the related tags can be helpful for linking data together in such cases.

Linked lists can also be built in similar fashion. For example, the miro user has imported the periodic table (with *about* tags of the form element:Mercury) and the planets of the solar system (with *about* tags of the form planet:Mercury). Each of these datasets form linked lists with tags ending -about being used to indicate the list structure, as can be seen from Figure 9-2. This makes it easy to walk through the list, particularly if they are viewed in a tool that understands these conventions such as the About Tag (*http://abouttag.appspot.com/monowing/about/element:Mercury*) web service.

Figure 9-2. An object representing the element mercury, with a link to the about tag for the next element in the periodic table in the tag "miro/elements/db-next-record-about"

Constructing About Tags for Common Objects

As we have seen, Fluidinfo allows any text to be used as a value for the *about* tag, and Fish (the Fluidinfo shell) allows direct specification of the *about* tag using the -a flag on most commands. Fish also incorporates the `abouttag.py` library, which can be used to construct *about* tags for various classes of common objects without knowing the details of each convention.

Fish provides three commands for constructing such standardized *about* tags:

abouttag
> Constructs standardized *about* tags for various kinds of common objects. The `abouttag` command can be abbreviated to `about`.

amazon
> Constructs *about* tags for books, albums, and tracks from the URL for such items on *amazon.co.uk* or *amazon.com*.

normalize
> Performs generic normalization for *about* tags, standardizing spacing and case and removing most punctuation.

The following sections discuss each command in turn.

The Abouttag Command

The general form of the `abouttag` command is

```
$ fish abouttag kind object-specifier
```

or

```
$ fish about kind object-specifier
```

where *kind* is (currently) one of URL, book, author, artist, album, track, film, isrc-recording, fi-user, fi-tag, fi-namespace, twitter-user, db-table, db-field, element, or planet, and *object-specifier* is a list of parameters that specify the particular object. These conventions are discussed on the About Tag (*http://blog.abouttag.com/2010/03/about-tag-conventions-in-fluiddb.html*) blog.

We'll discuss the command for each kind of object in turn.

- Web addresses (URL) can be specified through any of the strings URL, URI, url, or uri; they produce identical results. The URL normalizer standardizes URLs to conform to RFC3986 (*http://tools.ietf.org/html/rfc3986*), which includes trailing slashes on domains, removes default ports, and does various other things.

  Syntax

  ```
  $ fish abouttag url URL
  ```

Examples

```
$ fish abouttag uri FluidDB.fluidinfo.com
http://fluiddb.fluidinfo.com/

$ fish abouttag url https://FluidDB.fluidinfo.com:80/one/two
https://fluiddb.fluidinfo.com/one/two

$ fish abouttag URI http://fluiddb.fluidinfo.com/one/./two
http://fluiddb.fluidinfo.com/one/two

$ fish abouttag URL 'http://test.com/one/two/../?referrer=http://a.b/c'
http://test.com/one/?referrer=http://a.b/c
```

- Books and related items use the book-u (title, author) convention.

  Syntax

```
$ fish abouttag book title author-list
$ fish abouttag author birth-year birth-month birth-day
```

  As we saw earlier, there is already data on a number of books in Fluidinfo, particularly under the `miro` namespace.

  Examples

```
$ fish abouttag book 'Gödel, Escher, Bach: An Eternal Golden Braid'
'Douglas R. Hofstader'
book:gödel escher bach an eternal golden braid (douglas r hofstader)

$ fish abouttag book 'The Feynman Lectures on Physics' 'Richard P. Feynman'
'Robert B. Leighton' 'Matthew Sands'
book:the feynman lectures on physics (richard p feynman; robert b leighton;
matthew sands)

$ fish abouttag book 'The Oxford English Dictionary: second edition, volume 3'
'John Simpson' 'Edmund Weiner'
book:the oxford english dictionary second edition volume 3 (john simpson; edmund
weiner)

$ fish abouttag author 'Douglas R. Hofstadter' 1945 2 15
author:douglas r hofstadter (1945-02-15)
```

- Music-related items use `track`, `album`, `artist`, or `isrc-recording`.

  Syntax

```
$ fish abouttag artist artist name
$ fish abouttag album album-name artist-name
$ fish abouttag track track-name artist-name
$ fish abouttag isrc-recording isrc number
```

  The complete set of artists, albums and tracks listed in MusicBrainz (*http://musicbrainz.org*) has been published to Fluidinfo (over 600,000 artists, over a million albums, and over 10 million tracks), with data stored under the `musicbrainz` namespace.

Examples

```
$ fish abouttag artist 'Crosby, Stills, Nash & Young'
artist:crosby stills nash & young

$ fish abouttag track 'Bamboulé' 'Bensusan and Malherbe'
track:bamboulé (bensusan and malherbe)

$ fish abouttag album 'Solilaï' 'Pierre Bensusan'
album:solilaï (pierre bensusan)

$ fish abouttag isrc-recording 'US-PR3-73-00012'
isrc:USPR37300012
```

- Films use `film` or `movie`; both forms of the command produce the same results.

Syntax

```
$ fish abouttag film film-name release-year
```

Examples

```
$ fish abouttag film 'Citizen Kane' 1941
film:citizen kane (1941)

$ fish abouttag movie 'The Last Seduction' 1994
film:the last seduction (1994)
```

- Objects for key Fluidinfo objects include users (`fi-user`), namespaces (`fi-name space` or `fi-ns`), and tags (`fi-tag`).

Syntax

```
$ fish abouttag fi-user username
$ fish abouttag fi-namespace namespace-path
$ fish abouttag fi-ns namespace-path
$ fish abouttag fi-tag tag-path
```

Fluidinfo uses these objects for storing key information about Fluidinfo users, namespaces, and tags, under the namespace of the Fluidinfo superuser, `fluiddb`.

Examples

```
$ fish abouttag fi-user alice
Object for the user named alice

$ fish abouttag fi-namespace /bert/misc
Object for the namespace bert/misc

$ fish abouttag fi-ns bert/private
Object for the namespace bert/private

$ fish abouttag fi-tag γλαύκων/private/rating
Object for the attribute γλαύκων/private/rating
```

- Twitter users are normally identified in Fluidinfo simply by their Twitter username (handle) in its @-form. The command is very simple and simply ensures that the @ is present. Its general form is

  ```
  $ fish abouttag twitter-user username
  ```

  Examples

  ```
  $ fish abouttag twitter-user fluidinfo
  @fluidinfo
  ```

  ```
  $ fish abouttag twitter-user @fluidinfo
  @fluidinfo
  ```

  Twitter names that are obviously invalid will be rejected:

  ```
  $ fish abouttag twitter-user terry jones
  ```

  ```
  Fish failure:
    Twitter user u'terry jones' is not valid
  ```

  But there is no attempt to look up Twitter usernames from real names.

- Database components include tables (`db-table`) and fields (`db-field`).

  Syntax

  ```
  $ fish abouttag db-table tablename
  $ fish abouttag db-field field-name table-name
  ```

  These have been used to write structured datasets, such as the list of elements in the periodic table and the planets in the solar system by the `miro` user.

  Examples

  ```
  $ fish abouttag db-table 'elements'
  table:elements
  ```

  ```
  $ fish abouttag db-field 'name' 'elements'
  field:name in table:elements
  ```

- Miscellaneous objects are such things as planets (`planet`) and elements (`element`).

  Syntax

  ```
  $ fish abouttag planet-name
  $ fish abouttag element-name
  ```

  Using these conventions, there are objects in Fluidinfo containing reference data from Wikipedia on every element in the periodic table and on every planet (and dwarf planet) in the solar system, under the `miro` namespace.

  Examples

  ```
  $ fish abouttag planet 'Mercury'
  planet:Mercury
  ```

  ```
  $ fish abouttag element 'Mercury'
  element:Mercury
  ```

Finding Fluidinfo Objects from Amazon Product Pages

Storing data about books, music, and similar cultural items in Fluidinfo feels particularly natural. Although Fish's `abouttag` command provides an explicit way to locate the relevant object in Fluidinfo, it is often more convenient to locate that object somewhere on Amazon. Fish's `amazon` command provides a way to find the corresponding Fluidinfo object using the URL of a page on Amazon.

The scope of the command will probably increase, but today it works on Amazon US and Amazon UK product pages for books (including ebooks), CDs, and MP3 tracks. The form of the command is simply

```
$ fish amazon amazon-URL
```

where *amazon-URL* is the URL for such a product. Examples (at the time of writing) include

```
$ fish amazon 'http://www.amazon.co.uk/Hundred-Solitude-Gabriel-Garcia-Marquez/
dp/014103243X/ref=sr_1_1?ie=UTF8&qid=1307974975&sr=8-1'
    book:one hundred years of solitude (gabriel garcia marquez)

$ fish amazon 'http://www.amazon.com/Renbourn-Stefan-Grossman-Live-Concert/
dp/B000000E8R/ref=sr_1_7?ie=UTF8&qid=1308066155&sr=8-7'
    album:john renbourn and stefan grossman live in concert (john renbourn & stefan
grossman)

$ fish amazon 'http://www.amazon.co.uk/gp/product/B001KRSAKE/ref=dm_dp_trk1?ie=UTF8
&qid=1310939059&sr=8-6'
track:solid air (john martyn)
```

The reader may also be interested in the bookmarklet `az-fish` available from the top of Shell-Fish (*http://shell-fish.appspot.com*). If this is dragged to a browser's toolbar, clicking it while on a relevant Amazon product page will cause a redirection to the online version of Fish, where the *about* tag for the object should be shown.

Generic Normalization

Fish also offers more generic support for standardizing *about* tags. The `normalize` command simply performs some general standardization of text (as used by most of the conventions discussed so far), which involves mapping to lowercase, standardizing whitespace, and removing most punctuation. The form of the command is simply

```
$ fish normalize text
```

If the text consists of a single argument (which can include whitespace, if suitably quoted or escaped), the result will be a simple normalized version of that text. If multiple arguments are passed, the result will be joined into a longer string with the normalized arguments separated by colons.

Examples

```
$ fish normalize 'Tom Watson'
tom watson

$ fish normalize golfer 'Tom Watson'
golfer:tom watson
```

Command Substitution

A powerful feature of Unix shells is the functionality provided by the left-quote or *backtick* character. Quoting a subcommand this way causes the backtick-quoted command to be replaced by its output in the enclosing command. The output of several Fish commands is suitable for such use. For example, on Unix, Alice could show her rating of *Alice in Wonderland* by issuing this command:

```
$ fish show -a "`fish about book 'Alices Adventures in Wonderland' 'Lewis Carroll'`"
rating
Object with about="book:alices adventures in wonderland (lewis carroll)":
  alice/rating = 10
```

This example constructs the *about* tag for the book using the following left-quoted fish command, enclosed in double quotes (to keep it together):

```
fish about book 'Alices Adventures in Wonderland' 'Lewis Carroll'
```

The main source of complexity using this functionality lies in getting the quoting correct. In the example, we took advantage of the way Fluidinfo normalization strips apostrophes by specifying the title as `Alices Adventures in Wonderland`, omitting the apostrophe in *Alice's*. It can be included, however, with the slightly more complicated form:

```
$ fish show -a "`fish abouttag book \"Alice's Adventures in Wonderland\" \"Lewis Carr
oll\"`" rating
Object with about="book:alices adventures in wonderland (lewis carroll)":
  alice/rating = 10
```

Note how, in this case, the quotes for the inner abouttag command have been escaped using backslashes.

Fish also natively supports subcommand execution when used either from Shell-Fish (the online version) or from an interactive Fish shell:

```
$ fish
This is fish version 4.00.
> show -a "`abouttag book 'Alice\\'s Adventures in Wonderland'
'Lewis Carroll'`" rating
Object with about="book:alices adventures in wonderland (lewis carroll)":
  alice/rating = 10
> quit
```

In this example, the apostrophe is escaped with a preceding backslash, which itself has to be escaped because it is being used from a command within a command.

Fluidinfo Query Language Reference

Tag Presence: The has Operator

The has operator matches objects that are tagged with the named tag. For instance,

    has alice/rating

matches all objects to which Alice has attached her rating tag—all four objects in Figure A-1. Similarly,

    has γλαύκων/rating

would match only *Led Zeppelin IV* since that's the only object to which Γλαύκων has attached a rating.

 The value of the tag does not matter; even a tag with no value will be matched by the has operator.

Equality: The = Operator

The values of any tag having a simple native type can be tested with an explicit query of the form

    tag = value

where tag is the name of a tag and value is a specification of a matching value.

In the case of numbers, the operator tests exact numeric equality, so that both

    alice/rating = 5

and

    alice/rating = 5.0

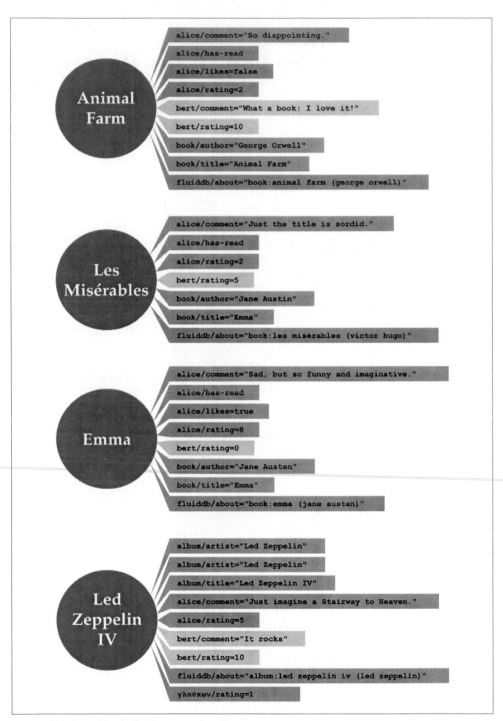

Figure A-1. Four Fluidinfo objects used to illustrate queries.

match any objects that Alice has tagged with a rating of 5 (or 5.0). String values will not match these queries (for example, tags with textual values "5", "5.0"). In Figure A-1 only the Led Zeppelin album, *IV*, will match.

In the case of booleans (true/false values), the words `true` and `false` will match, regardless of capitalization:

```
alice/likes = true
alice/likes = false
```

In the Figure A-1, only *Emma* will match the first query, and only *Animal Farm* will match the second query.

No numeric or textual values will match these queries.

In the case of strings, the = operator requires perfect matching including capitalization, accents, punctuation, and whitespace. The text to be matched needs to be quoted using double quotes in the query. For example,

```
alice/comment = "So disappointing."
```

will match *Animal Farm* in Figure A-1, but none of the following queries would match any objects

```
alice/comment = "So disappointing"
alice/comment = "Sö disappointing."
alice/comment = "so disappointing."
alice/comment = "So  disappointing."
```

because the first is lacking the final period, the second has an umlaut on the o, the third begins a lowercase s, and the last has two spaces between the words.

Null values can be matched using the keyword `null`, with any capitalization. For example,

```
alice/has-read = null
```

will match objects having the `alice/likes` tag with no value (or, equivalently, having a NULL value). In the figure, this would match all the objects except *Led Zeppelin IV*.

Tags whose values are lists of strings cannot be matched using the = operator, but there is a dedicated `contains` operator (see "List-Valued Tags: The contains Operator" on page 118).

 There is no "does not equal" operator. See the `except` operator, below, for one alternative.

Numeric Inequality Comparisons: <, <=, >=, >

Ordinary inequality operators can be used to match objects on the basis of numeric values. Floating point values and integers can be mixed. Boolean values and text values never match inequality comparisons.

Only objects having the tag used in comparisons can be returned. In other words, if an object has no `alice/rating` tag, it will not match any numeric comparisons on that tag.

In Figure A-1, the following numeric queries will match the objects shown below:

- `alice/rating < 5`: *Animal Farm* and *Les Misérables*
- `alice/rating <= 5`: All except *Emma*
- `alice/rating >= 5`: *Led Zeppelin IV* and *Emma*
- `alice/rating > 5`: *Emma*

Inexact Text Matching: The matches Operator

The `matches` operator can be used to perform various kinds of string matching. Its general form is

```
tag matches "value"
```

Assuming that the value given is simple (containing no spaces,[1] punctuation, or wild-cards), this will match according to following rules:

- Capitalization is ignored.
- Punctuation in the tag values is ignored.
- Whole words are matched.
- Accents are significant in the match; in other words, e, é, and è are treated as different, but é and É are treated as the same.

For example,

```
alice/comment matches "just"
```

will match *Les Misérables* and *Led Zeppelin IV* and

```
alice/comment matches "so"
```

will match *Animal Farm* and *Emma* (not *Les Misérables*, despite its containing "`sor did`", because only whole words are matched). Similarly,

```
bert/comment matches "it"
```

---

1. All "whitespace" sequences (substrings consisting of some combination of spaces, tabs, and newlines) are treated as equivalent by the `matches` operator

will match *Animal Farm* and *Led Zeppelin IV*; the exclamation point in the comment doesn't affect the match, but if we specify punctuation in the query it will, so that

```
bert/comment matches "it!"
```

will match *Animal Farm* only. This is particularly useful for matching *about* tags precisely. Thus,

```
fluiddb/about matches "book:"
```

will match the three book objects, but would not match an object with the *about* tag `the book of the dead`, if there were such an object in our example data.

If spaces are included in the query, instead of matching single keywords, the query will match a sequence of keywords, in order, with spacing being regularized both in the query and the tag values. This is called phrase matching. For example

```
bert/comment matches "I   love"
```

will match *Animal Farm* in Figure A-1, but

```
alice/comment matches "so imaginative"
```

will match none of the objects in the figure, because `so` and `imaginative` are not adjacent in Alice's comment on *Emma*.

The `matches` operator also supports two wildcard operators: *, which matches any sequence of characters (including none), and ?, which matches any single character. These wildcards work in keyword matches but not phrase matches. For example,

```
alice/comment matches "*is*"
```

will match the objects *Animal Farm* (`disappointing`) and *Les Misérables* (`is`).

Meanwhile,

```
alice/comment matches "so*"
```

will match *Animal Farm* (`So`), *Les Misérables* (`sordid`), and *Emma* (`so`), but would not match `also` if that were used.

Keyword query terms can also have a trailing ~ added to specify that Fluidinfo will do fuzzy matching, meaning that some misspellings and other similar terms will be matched. An example of such a specification is

```
alice/comment matches "imagine~"
```

which, in this case, matches *Led Zeppelin IV* (`imagine`) and *Emma* (`imaginative`), though giving a precise definition of what that will match is beyond the scope of this book.

Combining Queries with and, or, except, and Brackets

Complex query specifications can be built up using round brackets ("parentheses") in the natural way. For example

```
alice/rating > 8 and (fluiddb/about matches "book:" or fluiddb/about matches "album:")
```

will match books and albums Alice has rated over 8, which in Figure A-1 returns *Emma* only.

The except operator excludes previously matched objects that match further conditions. It can be thought of as subtracting the results of one query from another. For example:

```
(has alice/rating and has bert/rating) except has γλαύκων/rating
```

will match items that Alice and Bert have rated but which Γλαύκων has not—in Figure A-1, *Animal Farm*, *Les Misérables*, and *Emma*.

List-Valued Tags: The contains Operator

Fluidinfo tags can be lists of strings. For example, the musicbrainz.org user lists band members in this way:

```
$ fish tags -a "artist:led zeppelin"
Object with about="artist:led zeppelin":
  /fluiddb/about = "artist:led zeppelin"
  /musicbrainz.org/artist
  /musicbrainz.org/artist/end-date = "1980-09-25"
  /musicbrainz.org/artist/members = [
    "Jimmy Page",
    "John Bonham",
    "John Paul Jones",
    "Robert Plant"
  ]
  /musicbrainz.org/artist/name = "Led Zeppelin"
  /musicbrainz.org/artist/sort-name = "Led Zeppelin"
  /musicbrainz.org/artist/start-date = "1968-01-01"
  /musicbrainz.org/artist/type = "group"
  /musicbrainz.org/mbid = "678d88b2-87b0-403b-b63d-5da7465aecc3"
```

The query

```
musicbrainz.org/artist/members contains "Jimmy Page"
```

will match this object together with a few others (four, at the time of writing).

The matching is precise (capitalization, accents, spacing, and the like all matter). Multiple members can be matched in the usual way through using the and, or, and except operators, with parentheses as required. There is no way, however, to require an exact list match; we cannot specify that the list should consist of Jimmy Page, John Bonham, John Paul Jones, and Robert Plant *only*, or in that order.

Prior to version 1.14 of the API, Fluidinfo's composite primitive type was a *set* of strings rather than a *list*. There are two differences. First, lists allow repetition of elements (so that ["a", "b", "a"] and ["a", "b"] are different lists, whereas {"a", "b", "a"} and {"a", "b"} are merely different representations of the same set. Second, order matters with lists, but not sets, so that ["a", "b"] is different from ["b", "a"], but {"a", "b"} and {"b", "a"} are the same set.

This makes almost no difference within the query language (since only the `contains` and `has` operators are available for list-valued tags), but it means that where previously a list of strings sent to Fluidinfo would come back deduplicated, and potentially in a different order, both duplicates and ordering will now be retained.

Fish has changed to use square brackets rather than braces both for input and output as a result of this change to Fluidinfo.

About the Authors

Nicholas Radcliffe is a consultant specializing in predictive modeling and stochastic optimization. He is best known for developing *forma analysis*, a theory of representation for genetic algorithms, and *uplift modeling*, a novel statistical approach to predictive modeling as it applies in marketing optimization.

After earning a PhD in theoretical physics at Edinburgh University, he joined the newly forming Edinburgh Parallel Computing Centre in 1990, where he led a group that used high-performance computing to tackle business and commercial problems. In 1995, with three colleagues, he founded Quadstone Limited, a VC-backed company that built the Decisionhouse suite of analytical and visual marketing tools for large-scale data analysis. He served as CTO of Quadstone until 2007, when he left to form Stochastic Solutions Limited, a consulting firm that also develops and markets the Artists suite of analytical software. Radcliffe also serves as a visiting professor at the University of Edinburgh, attached to the Operational Research Group, and he has published numerous scientific and technical papers as well as the book *Sustainability: A Systems Approach*, written with Anthony Clayton for WWF (the former World-Wide Fund for Nature).

Radcliffe's connection with Fluidinfo dates back to the late 1980s, when he and Fluidinfo's founder, Terry Jones, both researched genetic algorithms, sharing a common interest in representation issues. Radcliffe has been a friend of and advisor to the Fluidinfo company since its inception. Radcliffe wrote the open source Fluidinfo Shell (Fish) software for interfacing with Fluidinfo, writes a blog, About Tag (*http://blog .abouttag.com*), that discusses representation issues as they affect Fluidinfo, and maintains several web services for accessing Fluidinfo. He also writes a separate blog on analytical marketing, The Scientific Marketer (*http://scientificmarketer.com*).

Nicholas Tollervey is a classically trained musician, philosophy graduate, teacher, writer, and software developer. He's been programming since 1984, when he taught himself BBC Basic at junior school. He currently works at Fluidinfo, where he gets to do all sorts of fun and exciting things, like trying to change the world of linked data. Prior to working as a developer, Nicholas was a senior teacher in an inner-city state secondary school in the UK. He has extensive experience working with students of all ages and abilities and still indulges his passion for teaching and learning by helping to run the London Python Code Dojo. A graduate of the Royal College of Music (he used to play professionally), Nicholas also has an MA in philosophy of education and financed his MSc in computing by writing reviews and articles for the UK edition of *Computer Shopper*.

Colophon

The animal on the cover of *Getting Started with Fluidinfo* is a jellyfish-like animal of the genus *Stephalia*. The genus encompasses three species (*S. bathyphysa*, *S. corona*, and *S. dilata*).

These creatures belong to the order Siphonophora, a group of marine invertebrates noted for its strange and striking members. Though they appear to be a single animal (like true jellyfish), siphonophores are actually colonies of intertwined specialized zooids. Some members of the order grow to enormous lengths (the giant siphonophore may be 40 to 50 meters long), others have severely venomous stings (such as the Portuguese man-of-war), and still others are able to produce light (which they use to attract their prey).

The cover image is from Lydekker's *Royal Natural History*. The cover font is Adobe ITC Garamond. The text font is Linotype Birka; the heading font is Adobe Myriad Condensed; and the code font is LucasFont's TheSansMonoCondensed.

Get even more for your money.

Join the O'Reilly Community, and register the O'Reilly books you own. It's free, and you'll get:

- $4.99 ebook upgrade offer
- 40% upgrade offer on O'Reilly print books
- Membership discounts on books and events
- Free lifetime updates to ebooks and videos
- Multiple ebook formats, DRM FREE
- Participation in the O'Reilly community
- Newsletters
- Account management
- 100% Satisfaction Guarantee

Signing up is easy:

1. **Go to: oreilly.com/go/register**
2. **Create an O'Reilly login.**
3. **Provide your address.**
4. **Register your books.**

Note: English-language books only

To order books online:
oreilly.com/store

For questions about products or an order:
orders@oreilly.com

To sign up to get topic-specific email announcements and/or news about upcoming books, conferences, special offers, and new technologies:
elists@oreilly.com

For technical questions about book content:
booktech@oreilly.com

To submit new book proposals to our editors:
proposals@oreilly.com

O'Reilly books are available in multiple DRM-free ebook formats. For more information:
oreilly.com/ebooks

Spreading the knowledge of innovators   oreilly.com

Have it your way.

CPSIA information can be obtained at www.ICGtesting.com
Printed in the USA
BVOW040254140312

285138BV00003BA/3/P